Y0-BSN-258

At Issue

Should the United States Move to Electronic Voting?

Other Books in the At Issue Series:

At Issue

Should the United States Move to Electronic Voting?

Diane Andrews Henningfeld, Book Editor

GREENHAVEN PRESS
An imprint of Thomson Gale, a part of The Thomson Corporation

THOMSON
™
GALE

Detroit • New York • San Francisco • New Haven, Conn. • Waterville, Maine • London

THOMSON
GALE
™

Christine Nasso, *Publisher*
Elizabeth Des Chenes, *Managing Editor*

© 2008 The Gale Group.

Star logo is a trademark and Gale and Greenhaven Press are registered trademarks used herein under license.

For more information, contact:
Greenhaven Press
27500 Drake Rd.
Farmington Hills, MI 48331-3535
Or you can visit our Internet site at http://www.gale.com

LIBRARY OF CONGRESS CATALOGING-IN-PUBLICATION DATA

Should the United States move to electronic voting? / Diane Andrews Henningfeld, book editor.
    p. cm. -- (At issue)
  Includes bibliographical references and index.
  ISBN-13: 978-0-7377-3882-7 (hardcover)
  ISBN-13: 978-0-7377-3883-4 (pbk.)
 1. Electronic voting--United States. 2. Elections--United States--Data processing.
 3. Voting--Technological innovations. 4. Electronic voting--Security measures--United States. 5. Voting-machines--United States--Reliability. I. Henningfeld, Diane Andrews.
  JK1985.S56 2008
  324.6'5--dc22

2007026024

ISBN-10: 0-7377-3882-0 (hardcover)
ISBN-10: 0-7377-3883-9 (pbk.)

Printed in the United States of America
10 9 8 7 6 5 4 3 2 1

Contents

Introduction

The presidential election of 2000 was one fraught with controversy. Neither George W. Bush nor Al Gore emerged as a clear winner for weeks after the November election, in large part because of problems with recounting paper ballots cast in the state of Florida. In addition, in other states, electors encountered problems with voter registration. Moreover, disabled voters continued to be unable to cast their votes independently and privately in most polling stations.

As a result, Congress turned its attention to reforming voting machinery and procedures, ultimately passing a bill called the Help America Vote Act of 2002. Generally known as HAVA, the bill requires, among other items, provisions for disabled voters, the elimination of punch-card and lever voting machines, and the creation of an Elections Assistance Commission. HAVA provides money to states and electoral districts to make the changes required by the law.

No one predicted the controversy or debate that the passage and implementation of HAVA would engender. Most people interpret the bill to mean that the antiquated punch-card ballots and pull-lever machines such as those used in Florida should be replaced with direct-recording electronic voting devices, known as DREs. These machines operate much as automatic teller machines do: A ballot appears on a computer monitor, and a voter registers his or her vote simply by touching the screen. Some of these systems include a paper trail, so that votes can later be recounted by hand if necessary. Many of the systems, however, do not although HAVA requires that all voters have the opportunity to verify their selections and change their ballots before casting them.

After the passage of HAVA, many states immediately began replacing their old voting machines with new electronic machines; by the 2006 mid-term election 38 percent of Americans voted on DREs. However, from the time of their first implementation DREs have been the subject of heated debate for a variety of reasons.

Individuals and advocacy groups protest against the use of DREs on the grounds that the machines do not accurately record votes. On the other side, voting officials and other experts contend that the DREs are far superior to paper ballots in accurately recording voter intention. In a press release dated November 3, 2004, Information Technology Association of America president Harris N. Miller said, "Electronic voting machines took an important test on November 2 [2004] and passed with flying colors. . . . We are gratified by the outstanding performance of this technology."

Another issue of debate is the reliability of the machines. Some voters experience difficulty in using the machines, and poll workers sometimes are not able to instruct voters adequately. On the other hand, many voters find the machines easier to use than the old machines. According to Conny B. McCormack's June 21, 2005, testimony to the U.S. Senate Committee on Rules and Administration, "overwhelming evidence exists throughout the United States that DRE voting systems . . . are accurate, reliable, secure, accessible, easy-to-use, [and] popular with voters."

A third point of contention is what is known as "auditability." That is, if an election is very close, how can election officials audit the vote if it is done on an electronic machine without a paper trail. Many voters and organizations call for the machines to be retrofitted with devices that would produce paper voter-verified ballots so that each voter can be sure that he or she voted for the candidate of his or her choice, and the paper ballots themselves can be recounted if necessary. Marc Fisher from the *Washington Post* writes on September 21, 2006, "people trust paper ballots because they're real. You can hold them in your hand and count them again if you need to." Proponents of electronic voting argue that the computer files provide adequate auditability.

Finally, many believe that the software used in electronic voting machines is not secure against attack from hackers, making elections vulnerable to fraud. In an article in *Salon*, for example, Brad Friedman, reports on a Princeton University study of a Diebold touch-screen voting system. According to Freidman, the study "confirm[s] many of the concerns often expressed by computer scientists and security experts ... that electronic voting—and indeed our elections—may now be exceedingly vulnerable to the malicious whims of a single individual." Others contend that paper ballots historically have been used to perpetrate election fraud. Michael Shamos, in his paper "Electronic Voting Records: An Assessment," argues, "the United States has been using direct-recording electronic voting equipment for well over 20 years without a single verified incident of successful tampering. . . . Every form of paper ballot that has ever been devised can and has been manipulated, in general with considerable ease."

HAVA mandated that all states comply with the new voting reforms by January 1, 2006. Many would agree that HAVA is good legislation. As Sarah Liebschutz and Daniel J. Palazzo write in the fall 2005 issue of *Publius*, "thus far, HAVA has positively affected election administration."

However, the controversies over accessibility, accuracy, reliability, and security of electronic voting continue, and by 2007, many states had not yet fully implemented the law. The issues raised by HAVA and the movement toward electronic voting promise to be at the forefront of debate for many election cycles yet to come. Should the United States move to electronic voting? It is a question that will continue to elicit the kind of debate found in the viewpoints of this volume.

1

Electronic Voting:
An Overview

Staff of the Institute of Governmental Studies Library
of the University of California

The Institute of Governmental Studies (IGS) Library is one of the premier repositories of information regarding political science and public policy in the United States. The IGS Library staff periodically writes overviews of important public issues.

Problems with voting procedures in the 2000 U.S. presidential election led to the passage of the Help America Vote Act of 2002 (HAVA), a key piece of voting reform legislation. HAVA provides money for voting precincts to move away from punch-card ballots to electronic devices. Those who think electronic voting is a good idea point to greater voter participation and greater ease of use with the new machines. Critics of electronic voting think that the machines do not work well, do not produce verifiable results, and can be hacked easily.

Problems with vote counting in the 2000 presidential election prompted a broad effort to upgrade voting systems across the country. The Help America Vote Act of 2002 (HAVA) is the key federal initiative in this effort. It provides funds, promulgates general standards for voter registration and election systems, and establishes an Election Assistance Commission to administer the law. The four members of the commission were confirmed by the U.S. Senate in December 2003, setting the stage for the regular disbursement of HAVA funds to the states.

Staff of the Institute of Governmental Studies Library at the University of California, "Electronic Voting—Overview and Issues: Introduction," www.igs.berkeley.edu, November 2005. Reproduced by permission.

Two Electronic Voting Systems

The central aim of the election reform effort is to move away from punchcard and lever systems to electronic voting systems, of which there are two basic types. Optical scan systems retain the paper ballot, which the voter marks with dots that are read electronically. Optical scan systems create a tangible record that can be used in recounts, and maintain consistency between ballots cast absentee and at the polls, but printing ballots is a complex and costly business. Touch-screen voting systems, also known as direct recording electronic (DRE) voting systems, dispense with the paper ballot altogether and operate much like an ATM machine, Touch-screen systems easily accommodate multiple languages and even have audio capabilities, making them attractive for meeting accessibility goals, but require a parallel printing system of some kind in order to provide a tangible record of the vote.

Major Electronic Voting Concerns

Both optical scan and the newer touch-screen systems have their advocates, but enthusiasm for them has been dampened by a range of concerns, voiced most strongly by observers in the computer science community. Most of the concerns relate to touch-screen systems, and they focus on:

- *Hardware/Software Reliability.* On the hardware side there are concerns that mechanical failures in touch-screen machines arising from electrical outages and other causes may leave votes uncounted or miscounted, with no means of recovery. On the software side computer scientists and others warn that software deficiencies in some electronic voting systems may affect election outcomes. Of particular concern are alleged flaws in software from Deibold, Inc., one of the major vendors of electronic voting systems. Critics note that vendor software is not amenable to outside testing because it contains secret proprietary code, and that vendors do not share the results of internal testing.

- *Verifiability.* If in a touch-screen system the record of votes cast exists only in digital form, there is no independent way to confirm that the votes were recorded accurately, and thus no way to conduct a reliable recount. Many observers contend that the solution is a voter verifiable paper trail, i.e., a print record of the voter's choices. In one proposal under wide consideration, the print record would be on a secure log that the voter could view on the touch-screen machine. The voter could confirm that his/her choices were accurately recorded, but would not have a personal copy of the print record. Section 301 of the HAVA legislation requires "a permanent paper record with a manual audit capacity," and states seeking HAVA funds will have to comply, but the specifics of the paper record are still to be determined.

  The paper trail requirement is not without controversy. Depending upon how it is implemented, the requirement may make elections more expensive, lengthen the time it takes to cast a ballot, and make elections more prone to delay and interruption from printer malfunctions. Many election officials voice these concerns, and note further that print records may be no more immune from post-election manipulation than old-fashioned paper ballots.

- *Security.* There is concern that touch-screen voting systems are not secure enough to prevent hackers from accessing voting data and manipulating results. A widely reported Johns Hopkins study noted that a voter could easily replicate and alter the smartcard used to program a particular Diebold touch-screen machine to "cast multiple ballots without leaving any trace." Critics claim that the touch-screen voting industry has been slow to address electronic security issues, and note that election officials lack expertise in the area. The situation may improve as standards and certification mechanisms for touch-screen systems improve.

Internet Voting Still Too Risky

Internet voting, i.e., voting on one's personal computer and sending the ballot electronically to the election office, has great potential for making elections more convenient and accessible, but concerns regarding verifiability and security are greatly magnified in the Internet environment, and there is consensus that Internet voting is at present too risky for general implementation. However, with continuing advances in encryption and other security measures, Internet voting is likely to become more prevalent, and Defense Department experiments and pilot projects are leading the way. In the interest of improving voting opportunities of overseas military personnel, the Defense Department conducted a pilot in the 2000 election called the Voting Over the Internet (VOI) Pilot Project, and planned a larger pilot for the 2004 election called the Secure Electronic Registration and Voting Experience (SERVE). Unresolved security concerns led officials to cancel the SERVE pilot in early 2004 before it was implemented.

In sum, views about electronic voting fall into two basic camps. On one side are those who put a premium on accessibility and improving political participation. They welcome electronic voting on the ground that its advantages outweigh security and reliability concerns—which in their view will always plague voting systems to some extent. On the other side are those who put a premium on security and reliability, and the need to maintain voter confidence in the electoral process. In their view, unless electronic voting is backed up with a verifiable record of some kind, the risks are too great—the potential for mishap and mischief looms too large.

2

Electronic Voting Machines Are Reliable, Accurate, and Secure

Sonia Arrison and Vince Vasquez

Sonia Arrison is the director of technology studies and Vince Vasquez is a public policy fellow at the Pacific Research Institute. Both Arrison and Vasquez are experts in high-tech public policy issues.

Direct-recording electronic (DRE) devices have solved many of the problems associated with paper ballots. The machines demonstrate few mechanical problems and they reduce voter error, making them more accurate than paper ballots. Because votes are tabulated quickly and precisely by machine, the use of DREs avoids human error. Although conspiracy theorists warn that DREs will lead to widespread voting fraud, no evidence to date supports this theory. Rather, the benefits of electronic voting are much greater than any risks associated with their use.

In the months following the 2000 Florida vote fiasco, federal lawmakers began work on new legislation to overhaul America's electoral system. The Help America Vote Act (HAVA) was signed into law on October 2002, allocating billions of taxpayer dollars to replace antiquated voting systems that have proven disastrous in post-election recounts. Nearly 700 counties have now procured direct recording electronic (DRE) devices, or "e-voting" machines, a type of cutting-edge technology that has quickly moved the country away from its perilous punch card past.

For millions of Americans, gone are the days of "dimpled" and "pregnant" chads. The use of touch-screen monitors and adaptable software has increased vote integrity and ballot security. With the click of a button, many Election Day errors have been innovated out of existence.

DRE machines promise to take voter enfranchisement to new levels. Elderly voters have found e-voting machines easier to read, a marked improvement from the small print and unpredictability of paper ballots. A majority of African-Americans have expressed a high level of comfort with DREs and thousands of handicapped voters, who sometimes were turned away from the ballot booth, have found new hope in the accommodating use of this electoral innovation. Indeed, e-voting machines proved critical to the success of the 2004 presidential election, which saw the rate of voter-ballot mistakes cut nearly in half from 2000 levels.

A 2004 Winston Group opinion poll indicates high voter confidence in the reliability of e-voting machines, and a strong understanding of their benefits.

Despite the advances made through DRE machines, prominent computer scientists have expressed concerns about the reliability and security of electronic voting. Some partisan advocates have attempted to make political hay from the discrepancy between the 2004 presidential election returns and Election Day exit polls. Further, Internet-fed rumors and conspiracy theories have sought to whittle DRE credibility with whispers of covert fraud and rigged elections.

Electronic Voting Is Secure and Effective

While the concerns of computer scientists are important, current evidence shows that electronic voting is more secure and effective than traditional ballots, which are more prone to human error and cheap fraud. Conspiracy theories have turned out to be just that. Post-election reviews have not found any indication of fraud or deceit involving the machines, and polling data suggests that the public is embracing the digital ballot box.

- A dozen different e-voting firms currently provide counties with various models of DRE machines, each using their own unique proprietary code, security, and access systems.

- On Election Day 2004, voters cast more than 40 million votes, nearly one third of the total, on approximately 175,000 electronic voting machines. Throughout the 2006 election cycle, over 65 million Americans will be able to use DRE devices at voting centers nationwide. Of the more than 27,000 "incidents" reported by voters to the Election Incident Reporting System (EIRS) on Election Day 2004, little more than 2,000 were related to "machine problems," which were not exclusive to DRE devices.

- A 2004 Winston Group survey found that voters using e-voting machines are just as likely to trust their voting technology as voters using lever machines and optical scanners. The survey further revealed that seven out of 10 voters were not concerned with the security of e-voting equipment, and that an overwhelming majority of voters who have used e-voting systems agreed that DRE devices are helpful in reducing electoral maladies, such as accidental over or under voting.

- A 2005 poll developed by the Pacific Research Institute found that 51 percent of Americans trust automated voting machines, with 25 percent not trusting, and 24 percent unsure. In addition, more than six in 10 respondents believed that new technology would help improve the voting process, and more than half said it would help reduce electoral fraud.

- Poll workers can be "professionalized" to reduce human error, and those with information technology backgrounds could be trained to handle more high-tech issues, such as troubleshooting DREs on Election Day. Partnerships between election officials and DRE device vendors could be forged to establish technical training programs for qualified poll workers.

- With a competitive DRE vendor industry, election officials can open a bidding process to meet any and all voter concerns for future purchases. Election officials and activists can track the outcomes of different vendor machines over time, compare their performance, and select those that best fit their county's needs.

The digital revolution has left an imprint on virtually every aspect of society, including the process by which Americans choose their leaders. On Election Day 2004, voters cast more than 40 million votes, nearly one third of the total, on approximately 175,000 electronic voting machines. Relatively few complaints about e-voting systems were received, and those that were could be attributed to user error. For the first time, thousands of handicapped and special-needs voters, who in the past have been turned away from their precincts, were allowed to vote at a polling booth.

A 2004 Winston Group opinion poll indicates high voter confidence in the reliability of e-voting machines, and a strong understanding of their benefits. Despite the overwhelming success of e-voting systems, the technology continues to be hounded by Internet-fed rumors and conspiracy theories of massive fraud and rigged elections. Perhaps surprisingly, prominent computer scientists and academics have come out against e-voting, and many have questioned the potential drawbacks of using machines at the polling booth.

Has America shifted too quickly from "hanging chads" to "touch-screen" voting, and is e-voting here to stay? This policy briefing examines the rise of e-voting, what its critics say, how to answer them, and what the future might hold.

The 2000 Presidential Election Recount

The widespread adoption of e-voting technology can be partly attributed to the problems surrounding the 2000 presidential election recount. With early reporting precincts handing George W. Bush a razor-thin Florida victory on Election Day, pundits called into question the notorious fallibility of punch-card ballots.

Within days, scores of lawyers and "chad teams" descended upon the Sunshine State, scrutinizing voter intent and wrangling the courts for control of the White House. For more than a month, accusations of minority disenfranchisement and voter fraud mired the state, leaving the country without a presidential successor. Having struck a major blow to the legitimacy of American elections, and voter confidence nationwide, congressional lawmakers jumped into action.

In October 2002, President George W. Bush signed the Help America Vote Act (HAVA), a $3.75-billion effort by Congress to overhaul voting systems and bolster voter outreach across the country. HAVA allows federal grants to be awarded to counties to replace outdated punch card ballots with high-tech voting solutions such as optical scanners and direct recording electronic (DRE) voting machines. Responding to complaints from voters who were wrongfully turned away from precincts on Election Day 2000, HAVA requires local election officials to create a statewide voter registration list, distribute "provisional" ballots, and increase polling access to disabled voters.

Republicans and Democrats alike have praised HAVA as a significant step towards fairer elections and more accurate vote counts. Representative Robert Ney of Ohio, the lead Republican HAVA sponsor, proclaimed that with the signing of HAVA, "no more will voters have to wonder if their vote was properly recorded or not."

Representative Steny Hoyer of Maryland, the leading Democratic sponsor, called the elections bill "the most important civil rights legislation since the Voting Rights Act of 1965." It is perhaps a bit of a stretch to place the legislation in that category, but nevertheless it makes it easier for counties all over the country to join the digital age.

A Comparison of Voting Systems

Most states have used their HAVA funds to replace punch-card ballots with Direct Recording Electronic (DRE) machines and optical scanning technology. However, not all of the voting systems of yesterday have been discarded in every county, so it's important to understand how they differ from the electronic voting experience.

Lever machines

Lever machines were a hallmark of early American voting, particularly along the East Coast, where they are still being phased out of existence. Under this system, voters pull levers on large machines to indicate their selections, which are then recorded by a mechanical counter.

Punch-card machines

Punch-card voting systems use either a stylus or a hole-punching mechanism to allow voters to indicate their ballot selections on a paper ballot. These ballots are then fed through reading machines to tabulate votes.

Optical scan ballots

With optical scan systems, voters fill in "bubble sheets," broken lines, or other types of paper ballots to mark their selections, which are then fed through an electronic device to tabulate the votes. Physical ballots are usually kept as an audit trail, in case errors, misfeeds, or miscounts are later discovered.

Direct Recording Electronic (DRE) machines

There are many types of DRE systems made by a number of different vendors such as AccuPoll, Avante, Diebold, Sequoia, ES&S, and Hart InterCivic. The specifics of each system vary, but one common method is to give voters personal identification numbers (PIN) or a "voter card," a credit-card-sized plastic memory card that they bring with them to access touch-screen or keypad-operated terminals.

After completing their selections, the machines present a summary of all votes cast. Voters are then allowed to submit their selections onto the official vote record, which is stored in the machine. After the election period has ended, each individual terminal is accessed with an administrator card and PIN, and the final count tabulated.

Nearly 700 counties in more than half the nation's states used DRE machines in the 2004 general election. . . .

DREs Are Accessible

One of the key reasons election voting systems have taken off so quickly is that HAVA requires recipient states to improve the accessibility and quantity of polling places in order to maintain eligibility for HAVA funds. This order includes providing polling booth access for individuals with physical disabilities, the visually impaired, and individuals with limited English proficiency.

Activists and leaders from the disabled community, including the American Association of People with Disabilities, are major proponents of DRE technology, as these devices are found to be more accessible to the handicapped than other voting methods. Special DRE features, such as Braille-embedded keyboards and headphones, enable the illiterate, the blind, and the physically challenged to vote at a polling location. In addition, DREs can be readily customized or retrofitted to accommodate the needs of a diverse electorate, without the cost of reprinting paper ballots.

Voters Trust DREs

Over the last 25 years, e-voting has been steadily increasing. In 1980, one out of 40 voters used DRE machines. By 2000, one out of nine voters used DREs. In 2004, one out of every three voters used DREs to vote. That is, on Election Day 2004, 40 million out of nearly 120 million votes were cast on 175,000 to 180,000 DRE machines. This growing use continues to build trust with the public. According to a study by Election Data Services, 39% of American voters—over 65 million—will have the opportunity to use DREs throughout the 2006 elections.

DRE devices provide two innovations to public elections: a visual verification of votes cast, and remote vote storage.

Poll numbers also validate the e-voting phenomenon in the country. A 2004 Winston Group survey found that voters using e-voting machines were just as likely to trust their voting technology as voters using lever machines and optical scanners. The survey further revealed that seven out of 10 voters were not concerned with the security of e-voting equipment, and that an overwhelming majority of voters who have used e-voting systems agreed that DRE devices are helpful in reducing electoral maladies, such as accidental over or under voting. Another survey taken later that year also found that the majority of African-Americans have a high degree of comfort in using DREs, more so than Caucasian-Americans.

The Benefits of DREs

DRE devices provide two innovations to public elections: a visual verification of votes cast, and remote vote storage. First, voters using e-voting machines are led to a screen where they are allowed to verify their selections; if the votes received by the terminal are incorrect, then the voter has the option to return to the contest in question and change his or her selection. Although HAVA requires all voting systems to allow voters to verify their selections, optical scanners and other methods merely offer verification brochures and printed reminders to double-check votes cast.

Second, votes are stored in each voting terminal, which can only be accessed with an administrative data card and password. Historically, paper ballots were overly manhandled, being placed into boxes, moved around, and passed through the hands of low-level poll workers to precinct supervisors and county officials. Fraud was less detectable, and more prevalent, as pre-scored ballots could be easily corrupted or votes altered with a simple punch through a hole, or mark of a pen.

The pre-DRE vote era was marked with a high level of trust and responsibility upon election officials, which due to innocent mistakes and malicious behavior, failed to completely secure paper ballot integrity. DRE devices have one of the lowest "residual vote rates" of any voting system because they help to reduce voter error. The residual vote rate is the total sum of "under votes" (no votes cast in a contest) and "over votes" (more than one vote cast in a contest) with a particular voting system. If a voter under votes on a DRE device, a user prompt pops up asking him or her to confirm that they are declining to vote. A similar prompt is used to prevent multiple votes, or over voting in a single race. Efficiency of e-voting machines is also an added benefit.

Electoral results with touch-screen voting machines are tabulated faster than hand feeding paper ballots through a punch-card reader or optical scanner, which may take hours, or even days to complete. Hand counts of paper ballots are prone to problems, as the repetitive nature of the activity and human fatigue draw less accurate counts than electronic or machine counts.

E-voting machines appear to have earned the confidence of the electorate, proving to be more reliable and easier to use than other voting systems.

DRE technology is constantly improving, and vendors continue to work to meet the needs of election officials. And with all the extra scrutiny being applied by computer scientists combined with experiments going on all over the country, Americans may wind up with a better-run election system. . . .

The Benefits Outweigh the Risks

As the famous American psychologist B.F. Skinner once said, "the real problem is not whether machines think, but whether men do." For years, conspiracy theorists and distrustful academics have warned of massive and malicious fraud with "black box" voting, but partisan pundits have yet to cite a single example of such activity. And it's not for lack of a paper trail.

A review of the voter-verified paper trail from an early 2004 election in Nevada found a complete and accurate record of the votes cast. Electronic voting technology made a major milestone in the last general election, as an unprecedented number of Americans used DRE devices to cast their votes. User error and poll worker mishaps with e-voting machines have been few and far between, and they are predicted to decline further with future use and familiarity.

At the end of the day, the future of e-voting lies in the hands of the American people. DRE devices will only become a mainstay in national politics if voters allow them to become so, and all indications lead one to believe that such is the case.

E-voting machines appear to have earned the confidence of the electorate, proving to be more reliable and easier to use than other voting systems.

The benefits appear to outweigh any risks that may arise with using electronic voting systems. DRE vendors have shown a strong willingness to work with election officials to quickly meet changing needs and requirements. The real question is how DRE devices and—later—Internet voting, will continue to shape the way elections are managed in America.

3

Electronic Voting Machines Are Not Likely to Be Hacked

Wayne Rash

Wayne Rash is a senior writer at eWeek. *He covers wireless technology and runs the Wayne Washington Bureau for* eWeek. *Rash is also a long-time columnist for* Byte *magazine.*

Voting fraud can take place with any kind of voting system, including paper ballots. In fact, mechanical voting machines were developed to prevent people from stuffing the ballot box. Electronic machines are even more secure than earlier systems due to sophisticated encryption software and increased physical security of the machines. Although it is true that any computer can be hacked by a dedicated attacker, it is not likely that a hacker would be successful in undermining an entire election. It is more likely that election problems will be the result of untrained poll workers.

On Nov. 7 [2006], a third of all U.S. voters will encounter electronic voting machines for the first time. As is the case in nearly any human enterprise that goes through a massive change, there will be problems.

There will be people who can't vote when they wish because poll workers weren't properly trained, or because somebody forgot some vital piece of voting equipment. Or worse, there won't be enough poll workers to handle the rush of voters, and things will just take a long time.

Wayne Rash, "The Real Problem with Voting Security," *eWeek*, November 6, 2006. Copyright 2006 Ziff Davis Media Inc. Reproduced by permission.

But what is almost certain not to happen is for the vote, any vote, to be hacked. This is because in reality, today's electronic voting machines are probably the most secure ever designed.

Despite the hysterical warnings of anti-electronic voting luddites [people opposed to technological change] and activist who yearn for a return to the paper ballot, it's harder to cheat on today's machines than it ever has been.

Missing Ballots in Past Elections

Forty-six years ago, during the presidential election of 1960, hundreds of ballot boxes containing thousands of votes on paper ballots mysteriously disappeared in Chicago during the supposedly secure transfer between the polling places and the counting facility. They were gone for hours.

When they finally showed up, those ballot boxes contained a victory to John F. Kennedy. The question that's frequently asked, but which has never been answered, was whether something happened to those ballot boxes while they were out of sight.

A dozen years later, while I was a young reporter for a television station in Virginia, I noticed that the board of elections had taken to reading the counters on every voting machine both before and after they were moved to polling places, and the machines were sealed each time. Why?

The jostling the lever-based mechanical voting machines took while being transferred meant that the counters sometimes changed themselves. Numbers would be different just because of mechanical stress on the voting machines.

At a few polling places in Florida during the 2000 election, optical scan ballots in some precincts couldn't be counted accurately. The ballots had to be counted by hand, delaying the vote count by a day, and introducing the potential for inaccuracy.

Vote fraud? Not exactly.

The county involved was trying to save money and was given the job for printing the machine-readable ballots to a printer with no experience printing such forms. The timing marks were every so slightly misplaced, and the ballots couldn't be read by the optical scan machines.

Confounding things, voting officials were doing everything they could to move away from paper ballots, if only because it was so easy to stuff ballot boxes.

All it would take is a loss of physical security for even a few minutes to swing a close election. And the loss of physical security for hours, as happened in Illinois, could result in a vote swing even in an election that isn't particularly close.

Enter the Mechanical Voting Machine

The solution for many localities was the mechanical voting machine. It might be cumbersome and prone to glitches, but it was hard to find a way to change large numbers of votes quickly. On the other hand, there was no way to tell whether that had happened or not. Mechanical voting machines had no audit trail at all.

But what voting officials did learn was that physical security of the voting machines was critical. Paper ballots and their easy-to-stuff ballot boxes were abandoned quickly except in the smallest communities.

It's no more possible to commit vote fraud [today] than it ever was, and in most cases, it's a lot less likely.

Voting machines of whatever type were stored in warehouses that were locked and usually guarded. The machines themselves had security seals applied, and the seals were checked any time the machines were put into use.

In addition, counters were checked and rechecked, and the machines were checked for proper operation.

So now it's 2006. More of the machines are electronic, and the only jurisdiction of any size still using the lever-style mechanical machines is the State of New York.

And suddenly, there's a cry about the fact that you might be able to hack the vote on an electronic machine. In fact, it has been proven that given enough time, computer scientists who had unfettered access to a machine, could eventually find way to insert bogus votes.

Election Voting Machines Are Not Easily Hacked

This should not be news. Given enough time, and enough access, any computer ever made can be hacked. But so can any other means of tabulation. Mechanical counters and paper markers can be handled fraudulently as well. There is nothing new here, other than the means of committing fraud.

The difference is that the voting machines on the market today use advanced encryption, they aren't connected to a network and most of them have a means to create an audit trail.

Even if a way were found to jigger a machine, say with a handheld computer, you're talking about a single machine. And even then the security software would report an event that would alert the election staff.

Sure, it can be done, but it's very difficult to hack the vote quickly or easily, and even harder to do it in large numbers.

In short, it's no more possible to commit vote fraud than it ever was, and in most cases, it's a lot less likely. Given the voter verifiable paper trails on 70 percent of today's electronic machines, it's probably almost impossible to actually get away with it.

The charges of the anti-electronic voting activists are playing on the lack of understanding by the media, the voting administrators and lawmakers to raise an issue that is, in short, bogus.

What they should be doing instead is focusing on an issue that's significantly more likely to be a problem, and that's poll worker recruitment and training.

Every person I talked to in researching a companion story to this column said they were worried that there wouldn't be enough properly trained poll workers to meet the needs of the voting public.

Instead of chasing imaginary charges of hacking the vote, local officials and others involved in this debate should be spending their time and resources on making sure the people who carry out the voting process know how to operate the machines, know who to call for help, and how to keep them physically secure.

It's not going to be hackers who steal the vote in this election. But it could be stolen by ineptitude and disorganization, especially if election workers are focusing on the wrong problem.

4

Electronic Voting Machines Can Be Easily Hacked

Jon Stokes

Jon Stokes, cofounder of the Ars Technica *Web site, is the author of* Inside the Machine: An Illustrated Introduction to Microprocessors and Computer Architecture, *published in 2006.*

The use of direct-recording electronic (DRE) voting machines makes U.S. elections highly vulnerable to attack at many points during the voting process. Computer experts have already demonstrated the ways that vote-stealing software could be built into the machines by dishonest programmers or introduced into unattended machines. They have also shown how DREs can be infected with viruses and how the central vote-tallying machines can be attacked. Any group capable of hacking an election and putting themselves into power could maintain that power forever; this is the greatest danger of electronic voting.

What if I told you that it would take only one person—one highly motivated, but only moderately skilled bad apple, with either authorized or unauthorized access to the right company's internal computer network—to steal a statewide election? You might think I was crazy, or alarmist, or just talking about something that's only a remote, highly theoretical possibility. You also probably would think I was being really over-the-top if I told you that, without sweeping and very costly changes to the American electoral process, this scenario is almost certain to play out at some point in the future in

Jon Stokes, "How to Steal An Election by Hacking the Vote," *Ars Technica*, www.arstechnica.com, October 27, 2006. Reproduced by permission.

some county or state in America, and that after it happens not only will we not have a clue as to what has taken place, but if we do get suspicious there will be no way to prove anything. You certainly wouldn't *want* to believe me, and I don't blame you.

So what if I told you that one highly motivated and moderately skilled bad apple could cause hundreds of millions of dollars in damage to America's private sector by unleashing a Windows virus from the safety of his parents' basement, and that many of the victims in the attack would never know that they'd been compromised? Before the rise of the Internet, this scenario also might've been considered alarmist folly by most, but now we know that it's all too real.

Thanks to the recent and rapid adoption of direct-recording electronic (DRE) voting machines in states and counties across America, the two scenarios that I just outlined have now become siblings (perhaps even fraternal twins) in the same large, unhappy family of information security (*infosec*) challenges. Our national election infrastructure is now largely an information technology infrastructure, so the problem of keeping our elections free of vote fraud is now an information security problem. If you've been keeping track of the news in the past few years, with its weekly litany of high-profile breaches in public- and private-sector networks, then you know how well we're (not) doing on the infosec front.

How to Steal an Election

Over the course of almost eight years of reporting for Ars Technica, I've followed the merging of the areas of election security and information security, a merging that was accelerated much too rapidly in the wake of the 2000 presidential election. In all this time, I've yet to find a good way to convey to the non-technical public how well and truly screwed up we presently are, six years after the Florida recount. So now it's time to hit the panic button: In this article, I'm going to show you how to steal an election.

Now, I won't be giving you the kind of "push this, pull here" instructions for cracking specific machines that you can find scattered all over the Internet, in alarmingly lengthy PDF reports that detail vulnerability after vulnerability and exploit after exploit. And I certainly won't be linking to any of the leaked Diebold source code, which is available in various corners of the online world. What I'll show you instead is a road map to the brave new world of electronic election manipulation, with just enough nuts-and-bolts detail to help you understand why things work the way they do.

Along the way, I'll also show you just how many different hands touch these electronic voting machines before and after a vote is cast, and I'll lay out just how vulnerable a DRE-based elections system is to what e-voting researchers have dubbed "wholesale fraud," i.e., the ability of an individual or a very small group to steal an entire election by making subtle changes in the right places.

So let's get right down to business and meet the tools that we're going to use to flip a race in favor of our preferred candidate. . . .

The Direct-Recording Electronic Voting Machine

There are many different types of electronic voting machines available from a whole host of large and small vendors, but this article will focus primarily on one type: the direct-recording electronic (DRE) voting machine. Nonetheless, optical scanners are vulnerable to many of the same exploits that I'll describe for the DRE; the only difference is that optical scanners leave a reliable paper audit trail that could be used to tell if an election has been tampered with, but such audits must actually be carried out to have any impact. . . .

How a DRE Works

1. The voter loads his ballot onto the DRE's screen by inserting into the machine the special smart card that he was issued by a poll worker. When the ballot screen appears, the voter marks his selections by touching the appropriate boxes on the screen.

2. The votes are read from the screen by the machine's vote recording software and recorded directly onto the DRE's internal storage, where they're stored along with the other votes that were cast on that machine.

3. At the end of the election, when all of the votes have been cast and are stored in the DREs, the contents of the machines' internal storage devices are then transmitted to the county Board of Elections (BOE) for tallying and archiving.

Note that the voter's choices are only recorded in one place: the internal storage of the DRE. Unlike the optical scan machines, the DRE system provides no permanent, nonelectronic paper record of the voter's intended choices that can be verified by the voter and then archived for possible use in an audit.

DRE Vulnerabilities

Now, the three-step process described above is vulnerable at multiple points in each stage. Here are just a few examples to illustrate what I'm talking about:

- **Step 1**: The machine could be tainted with vote-stealing software, or the voter could taint the machine with vote-stealing software by gaining access to it.

- **Step 2**: If the machine is tainted, then it can incorrectly record the vote. Or, if the voter has managed to make a supervisor card for himself, he can vote multiple times, delete votes, or disable the machine entirely.

- **Step 3**: If the centralized machine that does the vote tallying is tainted, then not only can it skew the election results, but it can also infect any DRE that connects directly to it, or it can taint any storage card that's plugged into it.

You might think that the supervisor smartcard cloning, viruses, and unauthorized accesses that I've described above are purely hypothetical. If the DRE in question is the popular Diebold AccuVote TS, then they're not at all hypothetical. All of the attacks that I just summarized, and many more, have been implemented by multiple teams of security researchers. . . .

Retail Vs. Wholesale Election Fraud

If we want to steal an election, then ideally we want as few warm bodies in on the scam as possible. All of the old-school election manipulation tricks, like voter intimidation, vote-buying, turn-out suppression, and so on, require legions of volunteers who know exactly what's going on; but in the new era of electronic vote tampering, an election thief can do a whole lot more with a whole lot less.

Election security experts break down voting fraud types into two main categories, based on how many bad apples it takes to swing an election: *retail fraud* and *wholesale fraud*. Retail fraud is the kind of election fraud that's most familiar to us, because it has been around for the longest time. In general, retail fraud involves multiple bad apples at the precinct level, carrying out any number of bad acts involving multiple voters and voting machines. Some examples of retail fraud are ballot stuffing, restricting polling place access by means of intimidation, vandalizing individual machines to make them unusable, counterfeiting ballots, and so on.

Wholesale fraud is relatively new, and it involves a single bad apple who can affect an election's outcome at the precinct, county, and state levels. . . . So with wholesale fraud, one bad apple can affect different barrels of various sizes, depending where in the election process she's placed. . . .

Manipulating Bits and Bytes

In conclusion, let me summarize what I hope you'll take home with you after reading this article and thinking about its contents:

- Bits and bytes are made to be manipulated; by turning votes into bits and bytes, we've made them orders of magnitude easier to manipulate during and after an election.

- By rushing to merge our nation's election infrastructure with our computing infrastructure, we have prematurely brought the fairly old and well-understood field of election security under the rubric of the new, rapidly evolving field of information security.

- In order to have confidence in the results of a paperless DRE-based election, you must first have confidence in the personnel and security practices at these institutions: the board of elections, the DRE vendor, and third-party software vendor whose product is used on the DRE.

- In the absence of the ability to conduct a meaningful audit, there is *no discernable difference* between DRE malfunction and deliberate tampering (either for the purpose of disenfranchisement or altering the vote record).

Finally, it's worth reiterating that optical scan machines are vulnerable to many of the same exploits as the DREs on which this article focuses. Optical scan machines do leave a paper audit trail, but that trail is worthless in a state (like Florida) where manual audits of optical scan ballots are not undertaken to clear up questions about the unexpected returns from certain precincts. I've been told that such audits are now prohibited in Florida by law in the wake of the 2000 voting scandal.

The State of Chaos

In researching this article, I talked on- and off-the-record with a number of prominent experts in the electronic voting field. The following e-mail response from computer scientist and e-voting/security expert Peter Neumann sums up the present state of chaos heading into the November [2006] midterm election, and it also communicates some of the frustration (and fear) that I heard echoed in the responses of the other researchers whom I questioned.

> The problem is much deeper than most people realize. The standards are extremely weak (1990 and 2002 both), and *voluntary*. The systems are built to minimum standards rather than attempting to be meaningfully secure. The evaluations are commissioned and paid for by the vendors, and are proprietary. The entire voting process consists of weak links—registration, voter disenfranchisement, voter authentication, vote casting, vote recording, vote processing, resolution of disputes (which is essentially nonexistent in the unauditable paperless DREs), lack of audit trails, and so on. You cannot begin to enumerate the badness of the present situation.

The clock is ticking on this issue, because a party that can use these techniques to gain control of the government can also use them to maintain control in perpetuity.

Paradoxically, the media blizzard of disparate facts, figures, vulnerabilities, acronyms, and bad news from a huge list of states, counties, and precincts, is in large measure responsible for the current lack of an all-out panic among the public and political classes as we head into the November mid-terms. This steadily roiling storm of e-voting negativity has resulted in a general uneasiness with DREs among the public and the media, but threat feels diffuse and vague precisely because there are just so many things that could go wrong in so many places.

A Ticking Clock

To get a sense of the problems that security researchers have in boiling all this bad news down into a single threat scenario that's vivid enough to spur the public to action, just imagine yourself travelling back in time to 1989 to testify before Congress about "the coming plague of identity theft." Or how about, "the rising terrorist threat from Islamic fundamentalism."

My own personal fear is that, by the time a whistleblower comes forth with an indisputable smoking gun—hard evidence that a large election has been stolen electronically—we will have lost control of our electoral process to the point where we will be powerless to enact meaningful change. The clock is ticking on this issue, because a party that can use these techniques to gain control of the government can also use them to maintain control in perpetuity.

5

Electronic Voting Machines Can Be Made More Secure

Michael Waldman

Michael Waldman is the executive director of the Brennan Center for Justice at the New York University School of Law. He was special assistant to the president for policy coordination under President Bill Clinton.

The U.S. electronic voting systems have both reliability and security problems. These systems, however, can be made safe through the use of voter verified paper records, audits of the paper records, regular testing of the machines, local control of voting software, and the banning of all wireless components in electronic voting machines. With these safeguards in place, electronic voting can be an improvement over earlier voting systems.

The Brennan Center for Justice thanks the Senate Committee on Rules and Administration for holding this hearing. We appreciate the opportunity to share with you the results of our extensive studies to ensure that our nation's voting systems are more secure, reliable and accessible. The Brennan Center for Justice is a nonpartisan think tank and advocacy organization that focuses on democracy and justice. We are deeply involved in the effort to ensure accurate and fair voting, voter registration, campaign finance reform and a reformed redistricting system.

Since the electoral debacle of 2000, the United States has broadly moved toward using new electronic machines to con-

Michael Waldman, *Testimony before the U.S. Senate Committee on Rules and Administration*, February 7, 2007. Reproduced by permission of the author.

duct elections. This is as wide a shift in voting technology as any in our history. The new systems promise fewer ambiguous votes (for example, in the case of Florida in 2000. "hanging chads" [particles of paper attached to a paper ballot by one corner]) and greater accessibility to the disabled. But they spawned doubt and suspicion, leaving many Americans uncertain whether their votes are securely cast and accurately counted. The issue became clouded in partisanship and conspiracy thinking, marked by conjecture and anecdote.

In 2005, in response to this widespread confusion and concern, the Brennan Center assembled a Task Force of internationally renowned government, academic and private-sector scientists, voting machine experts, and security professionals to perform the nation's first methodical threat analysis of the major electronic voting systems. The Task Force sought a simple goal: to determine, quantify and prioritize the greatest threats to the integrity of our voting systems, and to identify steps that we can take to minimize those threats.

Working with election officials, the Task Force analyzed the nation's major electronic voting systems for two years. It issued *The Machinery of Democracy: Protecting Elections in an Electronic World* (the "Brennan Center Security Report") in June 2006. The conclusions of the Brennan Center Security Report are clear:

- In fact, all of the nation's electronic voting systems—every single one—have serious security and reliability vulnerabilities (including especially, the malicious or accidental insertion of corrupt software or bugs).

- The most troubling vulnerabilities of each system can be significantly remedied; but few jurisdictions have implemented any of the key security measures that could make the least difficult attacks against voting systems substantially more secure. . . .

Fortunately, steps can be taken to make electronic voting systems substantially more secure. For the most part, they do not involve significant changes in system architecture. But they do require legislative changes—and resources, training, coordination and professionalization on a scale heretofore not known in American election administration. These changes can be made while assuring that our voting systems are fully accessible to all Americans. . . .

Recommendation #1:
Conduct Automatic Routine Audit of Voter Verifiable Paper Records

Advocates for voter-verified paper records have been extremely successful in state legislatures across the country. Currently, 27 states require their voting systems to produce a voter-verified record, but 14 of these states do not require automatic routine audits comparing the paper and electronic records. The Task Force concluded that an independent voter-verified paper trail without an automatic routine audit is of questionable security value.

By contrast, a voter-verified paper record accompanied by a solid automatic routine audit can go a long way toward making the least difficult attacks much more difficult. Specifically, the Task Force recommended the following audit measures, which, it concluded, would render attacks far less likely because they would force an attacker to involve hundreds of more informed participants in her attack.

- A small percentage of all voting machines and their voter-verified paper or audit records should be audited.

- Machines to be audited should be selected in a random and transparent way.

- The assignment of auditors to voting machines should occur immediately before the audits. The audits should take place by 9 a.m. on the day after polls close.

- The audit should include a tally of spoiled ballots, undervotes, and overvotes.

- A statistical examination of anomalies, such as higher than expected cancellations or under-and overvotes, should be conducted.

- Solid practices with respect to chain of custody and physical security of paper or other audit records prior to the audit of those records.

Recommendation #2: Conduct Parallel Testing

Although we strongly believe the best current security measure is to use voter-verified paper records as the basis for auditing the electronic record, steps can be taken to improve security should jurisdictions fall short of that goal.

For paperless DRE [direct-recording electronic] voting machines, parallel testing is probably the best way to detect most software-based attacks, as well as subtle software bugs that may not be discovered during inspection and other testing. For DREs with voter-verifiable paper trails and ballot-marking devices, parallel testing provides the opportunity to discover a specific kind of attack (for instance, printing the wrong choice on the voter-verified paper record) that may not be detected by simply reviewing the paper record after the election is over. However, even under the best of circumstances, parallel testing is an imperfect security measure. The testing creates an "arms-race" between the testers and the attacker, but the race is one in which the testers can never be certain that they have prevailed.

While a few local jurisdictions have taken it upon themselves to conduct limited parallel testing, we know of only four states, California, Georgia, Maryland and Washington: that have regularly performed parallel testing on a statewide basis. It is worth noting that California and Washington employ automatic routine audits *and* parallel testing as statewide countermeasures against potential attack.

Recommendation #3: Ban Wireless Components on all Voting Machines

Our analysis shows that machines with wireless components are particularly vulnerable to attack. We conclude that this vulnerability applies to all three types of electronic voting systems. Only two states, New York and Minnesota, ban wireless components on all machines. California also bans wireless components, but only for DRE machines. Wireless components should not be permitted on any voting machine.

Recommendation #4: Mandate Transparent and Random Selection Procedures

The development of transparently random selection procedures for all auditing procedures is key to audit effectiveness. This includes the selection of machines to be parallel tested or audited, as well as the assignment of auditors themselves. The use of a transparent and random selection process allows the public to know that the auditing method was fair and substantially likely to catch fraud or mistakes in the vote totals. In our interviews with election officials we found that, all too often, the process for picking machines and auditors was neither transparent nor random.

In a transparent random selection process:

- The whole process is publicly observable or videotaped.

- The random selection is to be publicly verifiable, *i.e.*, anyone observing is able to verify that the sample was chosen randomly (or at least that the number selected is not under the control of any small number of people).

- The process is simple and practical within the context of current election practice so as to avoid imposing unnecessary burden on election officials.

Recommendation #5: Ensure Local Control of Programming

Where a single entity, such as a vendor or state or national consultant, runs elections or performs key tasks (such as producing ballot definition files) for multiple jurisdictions, attacks against statewide elections become easier. Unnecessary centralized control provides many opportunities to implement attacks at multiple locations.

Recommendation #6: Implement Effective Procedures for Addressing Evidence of Fraud or Error

Both automatic routine audits and parallel testing are of questionable security value without effective procedures for action where evidence of machine malfunction and/or fraud is uncovered. Detection of fraud without an appropriate response will not prevent attacks from succeeding. In the Brennan Center's extensive review of state election laws and practices, and in its interviews with election officials for the threat analysis, we did not find any jurisdiction with publicly-detailed, adequate, and practical procedures for dealing with evidence of fraud or error discovered during an audit, recount or parallel testing.

Done right, electronic voting could be a true improvement in the way we elect our leaders.

In addition, the security of our voting systems would be enhanced by mandating good ballot chain of custody practices to ensure that ballots are neither tampered with nor lost, and by ending the exclusive private control that many vendors have over the code on voting machines owned by local jurisdictions and enabling those jurisdictions to access the firmware and software on their own voting machines. . . .

Voting Systems Can Be Protected

The Brennan Center Task Force found that the voting systems most commonly purchased today are vulnerable to attacks and that errors could change the outcome of statewide elections. This finding should surprise no one. A review of the history of both election fraud and voting systems literature in the United States shows that voting systems have always been vulnerable to attack. People have tried to "stuff the ballot box" since senators wore togas. Indeed, it is impossible to imagine a voting system that could be entirely, infallibly impervious to attack.

But straightforward countermeasures can substantially reduce the most serious security risks presented by the three systems. Jurisdictions with the political will can protect their voting systems from attack. The measures identified here—auditing voter-verified paper records, banning wireless components, using transparent and random selection processes for auditing, adopting effective policies for addressing evidence of fraud or error in vote totals, and conducting parallel testing—are achievable with effort. However it must be stressed that all these require human coordination. Our system of elections, run in 13,000 separate jurisdictions largely by part-time or volunteer officials, introduces numerous entry points for error, confusion and mischief. Fixing our electronic voting systems requires more than a technical fix. It requires a serious national commitment to election administration.

Do all the problems mean the United States should abandon electronic voting and return to paper ballots or other systems? We do not believe so. Paper is not a panacea. The other, earlier voting systems were rife with problems of their own, as we all recall. Done right, electronic voting could be a true improvement in the way we elect our leaders. Done wrong, electronic voting can create new opportunities for fraud, lost votes and inaccurate counts—all while diminishing confidence. So far, sad to say, America has not done this transition well. If Congress acts, we can move measurably closer to the ideal of every vote counting. The Brennan Center urges members of Congress to adopt these recommended measures as soon as possible.

6

Voter Verified Paper Audit Trails Will Make Electronic Voting More Secure

Rush Holt

Rush Holt serves in the U.S. House of Representatives as the congressman from the 12th District of New Jersey. On February 6, 2007, he introduced H.R. 811, a law that if enacted would require voter verified paper ballots in U.S. elections.

Democracy requires free and fair elections. Citizens must be able to publicly audit votes cast in elections. Electronic voting machines do not always provide a durable ballot for auditing purposes. Therefore, the United States should enact a law that would require a durable paper ballot for every vote cast; routine random audits; and countable emergency paper ballots in the event of machinery failure. The law should also prohibit wireless devices, Internet connections, and secret software in voting machines. These measures will make electronic voting more secure.

Chairwoman Feinstein. Honored Members of the Committee. I am Rush Holt. Representative from the 12th District of New Jersey. I am pleased to be before you today, and gratified that the Senate Rules Committee is again, and so early in the new Congress, holding a Hearing to consider this most critical topic in election reform—security issues relating to computer-assisted voting and what to do about them. When I last addressed this Committee in 2005, I noted that the coun

Rush Holt, "Focus on the Machinery of Democracy," *Testimony Before the Senate Rules and Administration Committee Hearing on the Hazards of Electronic Voting*, February 7, 2007.

try was suffering under the cloud of two controversial Presidential elections in a row. And now to that cloud we must add a Congressional race decided by 369 votes but with respect to which the votes of 18,000 voters went unrecorded for as-of-yet unexplained reasons.

Not only are the reasons unexplained: arguably, they are unexplainable. The software that counted the votes remains concealed, despite a dispute about whether it recorded votes accurately, and there are no independent voter-verified records confirming what the intentions of the voters were. The ballot is not durable. It is only a figment that exists in cyberspace. Democracy only works if we believe it does, and confidence in the process seems only to be further shredded with each passing election. Therefore again, I commend the Chair for addressing this critical issue so early in the Congress and I look forward to working with her to pass legislation to address this matter in the coming weeks so that the 2008 election will at last be an election we can all be proud of and confident in.

Votes Must Be Auditable

Free and fair elections are the very cornerstone of Democracy, and our elections can only remain free and fair if we, the citizens, can publicly audit them. Somewhere along the way we took a wrong turn, and handed almost the entire process over to the private corporations which sell us our "machinery of democracy." They sell us the machines, they sell us the software, they keep the software concealed, and they tell us who won. If we have a question about the result, they simply tell us that the software counted the votes accurately and we have nothing to worry about. I don't know what that sort of privatized counting and verifying arrangement is, but democracy it is not. The voter does not believe the voter is in control.

If a voter casts a vote on an electronic voting machine, verifying nothing but what is for a transitory moment in time reflected on the screen, how can the record of that vote be meaningfully audited? Can any election official, computer scientist, or voting system vendor reconstruct what that voter intended? No. The voter votes in secret. Because of the secret ballot, only the voter can verify that his or her intention is recorded correctly. That is why an independent paper copy of each vote—verified by the voter him or herself—must be required of all voting systems.

Votes are in a sense the "currency" of Democracy, and they are inherently valuable. Anything valuable, such as bank records, or property records, must be auditable. We wouldn't have it any other way. The same absolutely must be true of our votes.

I think it is worth considering how we took the wrong turn we did after the 2000 election—because we are the only ones who can safeguard our democracy and we must always ask ourselves whether we are doing that, and if not, why not.

Evidence of Voter Intent

Everyone remembers the 2000 election. In fact, at a . . . hearing on this issue in the Committee on House Administration, we were reminded of it graphically, as photos of election judges squinting at punch card ballots in Florida were displayed on large projection screens for all to see. Those, we were reminded, *were* paper ballots. Those, we were warned, would return us to the days of ambiguous evidence of voter intent and protracted disputes. Instead of removing the ambiguity from the record of each vote, many jurisdictions removed the record itself. In an effort to remove the problem of hanging chads [particles of paper attached to a paper ballot by one corner] many jurisdictions denied voters the possibility of verifying their votes and denied election officials the ability of ever knowing voters' intentions, and removed voters' confidence in elections.

In Florida 2000, at least we had evidence of voter intent. In Florida 2006, we have no evidence of it at all—or at least none that we are allowed to inspect. In Florida 2000, the election judges were able to make determinations about voter intent, even when the intent of the voter was not entirely clear. In Florida 2006, election judges cannot make any determination about voter intent because there is nothing tangible left that the voters themselves created or verified: whatever they saw on the touch screen, it was gone forever by the time the next voter entered the booth. All that remained was a software translation of voter intent, and a pile of unanswered and unanswerable questions surrounding 18,000 missing votes. Removing paper ballots from the computer-assisted voting process did not remove irregularity and fraud from the process, it removed the ability to discover and prove irregularity and fraud. . . .

Auditability and accessibility are not mutually exclusive, and should never be treated as if they are.

It is important to note that Sarasota County voters of every persuasion felt equally disenfranchised by the circumstances of that election. Voters from both major parties and a number of third parties joined together in a suit filed on their behalf by non-partisan public interest groups, not to say "I want *my* candidate to be declared the winner," but rather to say "I want to know *which* candidate was the winner."

That is the fundamental purpose of the legislation [H.R. 811] introduced yesterday [February 6, 2007] in the House of Representatives, along with more than 160 original bipartisan cosponsors. When the legislation is passed and implemented, we will always have the ability to audit results and conclude with assurance which candidate won.

Details of the Holt Bill

Although well-intentioned, the Help America Vote Act created at least one an unintended risk to the electoral system—it encouraged jurisdictions to purchase electronic voting systems at the same time mandating that those systems be independently auditable. My legislation would:

- Require a voter verified durable paper ballot for every vote cast, to serve as the vote of record in all recounts and audits;

- Require routine random audits in a percentage of precincts in every federal election, and an increased percentage of precincts when races are extremely close;

- Require that voters be given paper emergency ballots immediately upon machine failure, to prevent disenfranchisement; such ballots are required to be counted as regular ballots;

- Ban the use of wireless devices, undisclosed software and Internet connections to machines upon which votes are cast;

- Preserve and enhance the accessibility requirements of the Help America Vote Act and fund the development of new accessible ballot marking and ballot reading technologies;

- Authorize $300 million to defray the cost of implementing the paper ballot and accessible verification requirements of the bill; and

- Establish an escrow account through the Election Assistance Commission to create an arms-length relationship between vendors and test labs.

This legislation will strike the appropriate balance between the accessibility and the auditability of our electoral system, making a much-needed adjustment to the Help America Vote Act. Auditability and accessibility are not mutually exclusive, and should never be treated as if they are.

Support for the Holt Bill

The fundamental requirements of this legislation—a voter verified paper ballot for every vote cast and routine random audits as a check on the system—have been endorsed or recommended by the bipartisan Carter Baker Commission on Federal Election Reform, the non-partisan Brennan Center for Justice at New York University School of Law, the National League of Women Voters, Common Cause, People For the American Way, VoteTrustUSA, the Electronic Frontier Foundation, dozens of public interest and e-voting integrity groups the *New York Times*, the *Washington Post Roll Call*, the *Chicago Tribune*, the *Trenton Times* and many other newspapers. Our bill is very carefully drawn. Every detail of our legislation has gone through meticulous review not only by Members of Congress, but also by lawyers, Secretaries of State, public interest groups, advocates for voters with physical disabilities, election reform advocates, and civil rights organizations. In the 109⁰ Congress, a bipartisan majority of Members cosponsored it.

In addition, the country has done a veritable about face on this issue. When I first introduced this legislation in May of 2003, only a handful of states had a requirement for paper-ballot-based voting. Today [February 7, 2007] 27 states have such a requirement, and another eight used paper-ballot-based voting even though they do not mandate it. There are only 15 states that currently neither have such a requirement nor use paper ballot based voting, and it is time to bring those last few states into the fold so that all federal elections will be independently auditable. By the same token, only thirteen states currently conduct routine random audits, and the practice of routinely double-checking the accuracy of the results of computer-assisted elections too must become a national standard. This is not a partisan issue.

Time is of the essence. If we are to have confidence in our federal elections in 2008, we must act now, and work together to resolve any implementation concerns that may arise. Ensuring that our next general election will be independently auditable is by no means the only thing we must do to repair our electoral system, but it is the most time-sensitive.

7

Voter Verified Paper Audit Trails Won't Make Electronic Voting More Secure

Thomas C. Greene

Thomas C. Greene is the author of Computer Security for the Home and Small Office *and a regular contributor to the online periodical, the* Register.

Voter verified paper receipts give voters only the illusion of increased security in electronic voting systems, not real increased security. The paper trail only proves that the printer has reflected the voter's choice, not that the direct-recording electronic voting machine recorded the vote properly. In addition, paper receipts will cause a burden for both voters and poll workers because they will require voters to immediately review their paper receipt before the next voter can enter the voting booth. Therefore, voter verified paper receipts will cause confusion and delay without increasing security.

A couple of weeks ago, the US League of Women Voters incurred the wrath of touch-screen ballot skeptics by indicating its acceptance of DRE (Direct Recording Electronic) ballot machines with no voter-verifiable paper trail.

On 14 June [2004] following several days of bad press, the League revised its position and adopted a resolution saying that the machines should in fact be capable of printing out a summary of votes cast, as a protective measure against tam-

Thomas C. Greene, "E-Voting Security: Looking Good on Paper?" *The Register*, www.theregister.co.uk, July 7, 2004. Reproduced by permission.

pering and malfunctions. The decision was received with great praise from DRE skeptics.

Judging by the warm response, one might be tempted to think that the paper receipt is a security measure that will make e-voting safer from manipulation and fraud. Unfortunately, this is not the case, though it is widely believed.

Paper Receipts Provide the Illusion of Security

The voter's paper receipt has become the security *idée fixe* [fixed idea] of DRE skeptics, and a shibboleth [a word or phrase identified with a particular group or cause] identifying those who are on the "right" side of the debate. This is because the paper trail is a concept easily understood and conveniently communicated. It also likely derives much appeal from the fact that it involves an object that one can hold in one's hand and examine, unlike the results of a strictly electronic process.

There is no guarantee that the paper record will be the one recounted.

But it's far more security blanket than security measure. At the moment, there is so much wrong with DRE security that the paper record has become a harmful distraction.

Many things can go awry with a complex system like DRE, and a machine that spits out paper records can be every bit as insecure and prone to tampering as one that doesn't. But the piece of paper creates an illusion of enhanced security, which is why so many people insist in it. People imagine that, so long as the printout matches their recollection of votes cast, it's proof that the DRE machine is recording their votes properly. In fact, it's no such thing. It's proof only that the *printer* is recording their votes accurately.

There is no logical reason for a voter to assume that the printout in his hand, and the electronic tabulation in the machine, are the same. Numerous types of attack could produce an accurate record of voter choice on paper, yet still tweak the electronic results. And if the two results should differ, there is no way for the voter to know it. The receipt has no immediate diagnostic value. It can only tell a voter whether the data sent to the printer is the same data he recalls entering at the touch screen. The machine could well be rigged for a miscount, only with voter choices printed accurately. This sort of discrepancy would not be discovered until the electronic results are tabulated, by which time the damage will have been done.

The Paper Trail Causes Confusion

The only useful purpose of the paper trail would be to enable a recount using a different medium when there is reason to suspect the electronic results. However, for the printouts to be of any value in a recount, voters would have to review them carefully and note any discrepancies before the receipts are collected. Many ballots are long and confusing, so the idea that even a majority of voters would bother to scrutinize theirs is hardly guaranteed. And there may be numerous false alarms from people who, after confronting myriad races and referendums, may well forget one or two of the votes they cast and imagine a discrepancy where none exists, creating considerable alarm and delay.

On the other hand, if voters neglect to examine their receipts carefully before submitting them, they're worthless— there's no basis for trusting them more than any other result. A paper recount where perhaps thirty per cent of voters have actually bothered to verify their ballots is hardly the basis for confidence.

Furthermore, there is no guarantee that the paper record will be the one recounted. Many jurisdictions require that a recount be performed in the same manner as the original election, which might mean simply reading the machine's memory or storage devices again, unless specified by law. If local regulations don't require that the paper printouts be re-counted, there is little reason to collect them—except to create an illusion of security.

And if, during a re-count, some discrepancy between the electronic and paper results should emerge, the paper record would have to be paramount according to law to be of any use. Otherwise, there will only be confusion. But as we noted, unless voters are scrupulous about reviewing the printouts, there is no logical reason why they ought to be paramount. In fact, they probably should not be.

Paper Printouts will Become a Burden

The printout will become a burden on everyone concerned, including voters, because in order to be valid for a recount, the paper receipt would have to be free from marks and corrections. This is necessary to avoid the difficulties with interpreting voter intent that the infamous hanging chads [particles of paper attached to a paper ballot by only one corner] of Florida presented. With paper ballots, observer bias is a significant factor in determining voter intent. When confronting ambiguous results, such as pregnant chads [a bulging chad still attached to a paper ballot] and overvoting, Republican observers tend to conclude that the Republican candidate was chosen, and Democrats tend to believe that a Democrat was chosen. DRE criminals are designed to clarify voter intent, and, in theory, they can do this very well.

Imagine the delays caused by careless voters puzzled by their own choices, needing perhaps two, perhaps three, turns at the terminal to get things right.

However, if the paper receipt is to be used in a recount, it would be necessary for each voter to review it before the next voter would be allowed to use the terminal. Thus, if there are discrepancies, the voter's results could be cleared from the terminal, and they would have another go. This would be necessary so that, in the end, the voter can submit a "clean" receipt: one free of marks and corrections, to avoid a re-run of the chad debacle. A security protocol would have to be devised to ensure that the disputed receipt is disposed of properly and the voter-approved one substituted, without breaching voter privacy.

Furthermore, if it were possible for one person to clear any result from a DRE terminal, this would be a monumental security hole in itself. Thus it would be necessary for two election supervisors (preferably with different party affiliations) to perform the electronic equivalent of turning the keys needed to launch a nuclear missile, perhaps with different passwords, or with two smart cards, or some means of authentication along those lines.

Imagine the delays caused by careless voters puzzled by their own choices, needing perhaps two, perhaps three, turns at the terminal to get things right. And let's not forget that "getting things right" in this context means only that the printout matches the voter's own recollection of what they did at the terminal. The paper receipts will add not one shred of security, but they will bring about confusion and delays and Florida-esque disputes.

8

Voter Verified Paper Audit Trails Are Necessary for Accurate Elections

David Dill

David Dill is a professor of computer science at Stanford University. He is also the founder of the Verified Voting Foundation and VerifiedVoting.org

Because electronic voting systems are prone to tampering, breakdown, and programming errors, they must be equipped with voter verified paper audit trails to ensure election accuracy and integrity. Precinct-based, optical-scan ballots and touch-screen machines that print paper ballots provide the paper trail necessary to carry out recounts. Ballot recounts must be conducted regularly to verify electronic election results. Voter confidence depends on both on voter verified paper ballots as well as on regular auditing of the vote.

As a result of problems with elections in recent years, funding is being made available at all levels of government to upgrade election equipment. Unfortunately, some of the equipment being purchased, while superficially attractive to both voters and election officials, poses unacceptable risks to election integrity—risks of which election officials and the general public are largely unaware.

We are in favor of the use of technology to solve difficult problems, but we know that technology must be used appro-

David Dill, "Resolution on Electronic Voting," *Verified Voting Foundation.* www.veri fiedvotingfoundation.org, Reproduced by permission.

priately, with due attention to associated risks. For those who need to upgrade, there are safe, cost-effective alternatives available right now, and the potential for vastly better ones in the future. For these reasons, we endorse the following resolution:

> Computerized voting equipment is inherently subject to programming error, equipment malfunction, and malicious tampering. It is therefore crucial that voting equipment provide a voter-verifiable audit trail, by which we mean a permanent record of each vote that can be checked for accuracy by the voter before the vote is submitted, and is difficult or impossible to alter after it has been checked. Many of the electronic voting machines being purchased do not satisfy this requirement. Voting machines should not be purchased or used unless they provide a voter-verifiable audit trail; when such machines are already in use, they should be replaced or modified to provide a voter-verifiable audit trail. Providing a voter-verifiable audit trail should be one of the essential requirements for certification of new voting systems.

We elaborate below.

The Problem with Direct-Recording Electronic Voting Machines

In response to the need to upgrade outdated election systems, many states and communities are considering acquiring "Direct Recording Electronic" (DRE) voting machines (such as "touch-screen voting machines" mentioned frequently in the press). Some have already acquired them. Unfortunately, there is insufficient awareness that these machines pose an unacceptable risk that errors or deliberate election-rigging will go undetected, since they do not provide a way for the voters to verify independently that the machine correctly records and counts the votes they have cast. Moreover, if problems are detected after an election, there is no way to determine the correct outcome of the election short of a revote. Deployment of new voting machines that do not provide a voter-verifiable audit trail should be halted, and existing machines should be replaced or modified to produce ballots that can be checked independently by the voter before being submitted, and cannot be altered after submission. These ballots would count as the actual votes, taking precedence over any electronic counts.

When a reasonably reliable, accurate, and secure voting technology is already in use, such as optical scan ballots, acquisition of DRE machines would be a major step backwards.

Election integrity cannot be assured without openness and transparency. But an election without voter-verifiable ballots cannot be open and transparent: The voter cannot know that the vote eventually reported is the same as the vote cast, nor can candidates or others gain confidence in the accuracy of the election by observing the voting and vote counting processes.

Electronic Voting Causes Questionable Elections

All computer systems are subject to subtle errors. Moreover, computer systems can be deliberately corrupted at any stage of their design, manufacture, and use. The methods used to do this can be extremely difficult to foresee and detect. Current standards and procedures for certifying electronic election equipment do not require unambiguously that equipment provide a voter-verifiable audit trail. Without a voter-verifiable audit trail, it is not practical to provide reasonable assurance of the integrity of these voting systems by any combination of design review, inspection, testing, logical analysis, or control of the system development process. For example, a programmer working for the machine vendor could modify the machine software to mis-record a few votes for party A as votes for party B, and this change could be triggered only during the actual election, not during testing. Many computer scientists could list dozens of other plausible ways to compromise computerized voting machines.

Most importantly, there is no reliable way to detect errors in recording votes or deliberate election rigging with these machines. Hence, the results of any election conducted using these machines are open to question.

Available Alternatives to DRE Machines

When a reasonably reliable, accurate, and secure voting technology is already in use, such as optical scan ballots, acquisition of DRE machines would be a major step backwards. However, many areas urgently need to upgrade their equipment before the 2004 elections. In these cases there are several acceptable options available now.

Unauditable voting equipment will erode confidence in our elections, causing further disillusionment of the voting public.

At this time, the only tried-and-true technology for providing a voter-verified audit trail is a paper ballot, where the votes recorded can be easily read and checked by the voter. With appropriate election administration policies (for example, ensuring the physical security of ballots), voters can be reasonably confident of the integrity of election results. Two specific alternatives that are available now are:

- *Precinct-based optical scan ballots.* The CalTech/MIT Voting Technology Project found them to be the most accurate at recording the voter's intent and not significantly more expensive per vote than touch-screen machines.

- *Touch screen machines that print paper ballots.* Such systems would have many of the advantages of DRE machines, including potentially improved accessibility for voters with disabilities. There is at least one such machine that is certified in several states, and we hope that all vendors of existing DRE machines could provide an option to add ballot printers (DRE voting machines in Brazil have been retrofitted with ballot printers, for example). The paper ballots must be submitted by the voters, to be available for counting or recounting and to avoid vote-selling. The votes on the paper ballots must be regarded as the definitive legal votes, taking precedence over electronic records or counts.

Of course, use of appropriate equipment is not sufficient to guarantee election integrity. Elections must be administered to minimize the possibility of error and fraud, and maximize the likelihood of detecting them if they occur. In particular, even with an audit trail, audits must actually be conducted. If electronic counts are used from machines that also print ballots, or if paper ballots are counted electronically, manual recounts must be conducted with enough frequency to make the detection of error or fraud likely.

Electronic Voting Erodes Voter Confidence

There is certainly room for improvement in voting technology. Elections pose several unique technological challenges, especially simultaneously achieving auditability while preserving ballot secrecy. Voting technology is an active research area that has already produced several proposals that promise to be much better than any system currently in use. For example, there are proposals that may be able to eliminate the possibility of "ballot box stuffing." Unfortunately, if available funds are spent on fatally-flawed "high-tech" voting equipment, it will be a long time before there is more funding to adopt truly superior voting technology.

The conduct of elections has been taken for granted for too long. Election reform is now receiving much-needed attention, but we must guard against changes that inadvertently create even worse problems. Unauditable voting equipment will erode confidence in our elections, causing further disillusionment of the voting public.

9

Direct Recording Electronic Voting Systems Are Accessible for the Disabled

Jim Dickson

Jim Dickson is the president of government affairs at the American Association of People with Disabilities (AAPD) and is also blind. He leads the AAPD Disability Vote Project.

Before the passage of the 2002 Help America Vote Act (HAVA), disabled people often had to rely on others to cast their votes. HAVA and new technology have changed this. Direct-recording electronic (DRE) voting machines are accessible for disabled people and trusted by most Americans. DREs make it possible for the disabled to cast their ballots privately and independently, as required by HAVA. Requiring voters to verify their votes with paper will not improve accuracy and will make voting inaccessible for disabled people.

The US Census reports that there are 10 million Americans whose vision interferes with their ability to read print. There are millions more who cannot read print because their disability prevents them from handling paper. There are thousands of brave and dedicated Americans who have recently been disabled by defending this country. All of us want to thank Congress for passing the Help Americans Vote Act (HAVA). For the first time, because of this Act, millions of us have experienced the awesome wonder that comes with cast-

Jim Dickson, *Verification, Security, and Paper Trails: Testimony before the U.S. House of Representatives' Committee on Administration, Hearings on Electronic Voting Machines*, September 28, 2006. Reproduced by permission of the author.

ing a secret ballot. I've been voting for 39 years. The last two elections are the only elections where I have cast a secret ballot. Prior to the passage of HAVA, millions of us have had to trust others to mark our ballot. I want to report to you some experiences in the polling place which happened to me. Keep in mind that these type of experiences have happened to millions of our fellow citizens.

Voting Experiences of the Disabled

My wife and I made history when we became the first married couple to disagree on who to vote for. As she marked my ballot she said, "Vote Jim. I know you love me now. I know you trust me because you think I'm marking this ballot for that idiot." [Jim Dickson is blind.]

The very first time I voted, a poll worker assisted. When I told her my choice for President she said, "YOU want to vote for WHO?" She said this loud enough for everyone in the polling place to hear. On another occasion a poll worker was assisting me and she said, referring to state legislative races, "Nobody votes for these people, so let's stop here." On another occasion a poll worker said to me, "the referenda are confusing and long so it's alright if I don't read them to you, okay?" On a different occasion I had a poll worker say to me, "the print on these referenda is too small for me to see"—a comment that did not get much sympathy from me.

Independent testing authorities have tested DREs against federally-issued standards.

Other AAPD [American Association of People with Disabilities] members have written to me about their joy in voting independently for the first time. One wrote, "I always thought I was an American citizen. The day I cast my first secret ballot, I knew that I am an American citizen." Another member wrote that, "Isn't voting independently what my dear

America is about? Isn't that what equality is intended to be?" This member then went on to write, "If you want to make my day, just ask me who I voted for."

AAPD's Principles

AAPD has developed a statement of Principles on Accessible Voting. It reads:

> Full participation in American society must include full access to voting in all its aspects, on an equal and independent basis. Election Day is one day when every American is free and must be equal. Election Day is one day when every American is measured by their willing participation in American democracy.
>
> Individuals with disabilities must be able to participate fully and equally in American democracy.
>
> AAPD supports voting systems that are accessible, secure, accurate and recountable.
>
> The Help America Vote Act (HAVA) requires that voting systems be accessible to voters with disabilities "in a manner that provides the same opportunity for access and participation (including privacy and independence) as for other voters."
>
> This section of the law encapsulates AAPD's position regarding accessible voting. Voting access applies to the entire voting system. A voting system provides these distinct and equally important processes: making one's selections, verifying one's selections, and casting one's vote.
>
> Voters with disabilities must be able to do each part, privately and independently.
>
> HAVA mandates that the requirement for private and independent voting must be met by January 1, 2006, through the use of one direct recording electronic (DRE) voting system

or other device at each polling place. A DRE is a computerized voting device often called a touchscreen. Congress has set the date for compliance as January 1, 2006, and the US Attorney General does not have the legal authority to extend this deadline. Jurisdictions must meet this deadline. Election officials, voting machine manufacturers and others have known of this deadline for almost three years. The United States Department of Justice has repeatedly pointed this out both in writing and in presentations before numerous conferences of election officials.

Independent testing authorities have tested DREs against federally-issued standards. Jurisdictions must purchase voting systems, at least one per polling place, that provide independent and private voting that includes all three steps in the voting process: making one's selections, verifying one's selections, and casting one's vote.

AAPD will work to ensure that HAVA's accessibility requirements are implemented in a timely manner in jurisdictions across the US.

Missed Deadlines

Unfortunately half the country has missed the law's implementation of January 1, 2006 deadline. In Elections Data Services, a report commissioned by the EAC [Election Assistance Commission], states that in this November's election 39% of voters will be voting on accessible voting equipment. This represents 34% of the nation's voting jurisdictions. The rest of the country has either not purchased accessible voting equipment or purchased or leased equipment which claims to be accessible but which compared to other products denies a secret ballot to millions of Americans. The counties that have failed to meet HAVA's implementation deadline all use as an excuse the supposed need for a voter verified paper trail. The clamor for a paper trail actually comes from a very loud and very small segment of the country.

Over the past few years there have been several public opinion polls asking Americans of voting age if they have confidence that their vote will be counted on a touchscreen voting system. These polls have been commissioned by news media, independent investigators and election officials. In every survey that I am aware of, in the neighborhood of 80% of Americans have confidence and trust in touchscreen voting.

This summer [2006] a poll commissioned by the Election Science Institute again reports that roughly 80% of Americans trust touchscreen voting to accurately count their vote.

A paper ballot including a paper trail is not accessible.

You have heard that more than 25 states have passed legislation requiring a paper trail. Looking at the details of that legislation, nearly half of the states have legislation where the paper trail is not the ballot of record. This is for very good reasons. We have a long and painful history in our country of fraud and manipulation on counting paper ballots.

Paper Ballots Are Not Accessible

A paper ballot including a paper trail is not accessible. Millions of Americans cannot read it or handle it. Advocates for papers trails claim that there are paper trail systems that are accessible. These advocates have expertise in computers, not disability. They claim that so-called ballot marking devices are accessible. There are 2005 voting system guidelines issued by the EAC that require if there is to be a paper trail on touchscreen, the paper trail must be accessible. Such a machine does not exist and such a machine has not been certified by the EAC. When and if such a machine exists and there is federal funds to pay for it, the inaccessible problems with the paper trail would go away. It is a very large *if* there will be federal funds and the paper trail advocates conveniently ignore the time it will take to develop, test, certify and deploy an accessible paper trail. Let's look at the underlying assumptions regarding the desirability of paper ballots. Recently there was an attempt to count the paper trail ballots from Cleveland's May primary. Ten percent of ballots were not countable. Thank god it was not a close election and that there was no need for a re-count. Under Ohio law the paper is the ballot and given that misguided law, the 10% of citizens whose votes were re-corded on touchscreen would not have their votes counted in a re-count.

There is a false assumption that huge numbers of paper ballots can be accurately re-counted. Accurate paper ballot re-counts can be done but only on counting in the tens of thousands. In an MIT experiment for every 10,000 ballots counted, there are 3 errors. In the 2004 governor's race in Washington State, 1.98 million votes were on paper. The paper was re-counted three times. Each time it was counted there were different totals. Re-counts of paper ballots in very close elections always result in doubt as to who won, accusations of fraud and manipulation. How does changing the result of a re-count build confidence and trust in our elections?

Paper Verification Is Inaccurate

Voters including voters with disability have the right to verify their ballot. It turns out that verifying on a piece of paper does not happen. Most voters do not look. In an experiment at MIT, visual verification of a paper ballot was compared to audio verification of a ballot. The experiment was set up so that the touchscreen actually changed the vote on the paper from the voter's intent. MIT undergraduate and graduate students participated in this study. Even when the paper trail printed a changed vote, a significant number of the students did not observe change. When the verification was done with earphones, a significantly greater number of students found the changed vote.

To summarize, voter verified paper trails attached to accessible touchscreens are not accessible and it will be years before such projects can legally be purchased—assuming that there will be hundreds of millions of dollars to buy them. In the real world of human beings voting, paper trails verification is a Rub[e] Goldberg [cartoonist famed for drawing complex machines to perform simple tasks] contraption. In close elections with millions of paper ballots it is impossible to know for certain who won. Voters do not verify, voters don't use it, and large numbers of voters will fail should there be a security attack. Most voters will not recognize the change on the paper ballot. Before the Congress requires a verification system, we need to be certain that the verification system allows for accurate recounts, will be used by voters and that the verification system is accessible. Before Congress requires that something be placed into the sanctity of the voting booth, Congress should support a rigorous testing.

10

Direct Recording Electronic Voting Systems Not Accessible for Disabled

Noel H. Runyan

Noel H. Runyan is a computer scientist and engineer who is also blind. He actively works to increase accessibility for voters with disabilities.

Voters with disabilities increasingly find that direct-recording electronic (DRE) voting systems do not provide either adequate accessibility or security. Further, the labs charged with testing the devices for accessibility have failed in this responsibility. Although DREs held the promise that disabled voters would be able to cast their votes independently and privately, the devices are so poorly designed that few disabled people find them accessible.

Originally, people with disabilities were not considered to be qualified to vote. Eventually, they were permitted to vote but were forced to allow election officials in the voting booth. For decades now, most states have allowed a personal choice of assistant to help in the voting booth.

With the passage of the Help America Vote Act [2002], the goal of privacy and access for all voters with disabilities, as well as an end to hanging chad and over- and undervoting, seemed within reach.

Vendors began showing primitively modified prototype "accessible" voting systems. The computer interfaces on some

Noel H. Runyan, *Improving Access to Voting*. New York: Demos, 2007. Reproduced by permission.

of these new machine prototypes allowed some voters who were blind to vote successfully with audio output and tactile control keys. These new direct-recording electronic (DRE) voting systems seemed to hold a great deal of promise for reliable and accessible voting. This encouraged many to become vocal advocates of DRE voting systems. The National Federation of the Blind (NFB) and others strongly pushed for DREs in order to "hurry up and get accessible voting for the blind."

Today, the goal of private and independent voting has been achieved by some voters with disabilities. But many others have been disappointed and frustrated because they have not been able to vote privately and independently as they had hoped and as voting-system vendors had promised.

DREs Do Not Live Up to Their Promise

As this paper details, many of the DREs in use today do not fulfill the promise of accessibility for the majority of voters with disabilities.

Because HAVA encouraged the purchase of DRE voting systems on the grounds that they were supposed to be accessible, they are now prevalent throughout the United States. As DRE security problems surfaced publicly, voter-verifiable paper audit trails (VVPATs) were proposed as the security "fix." Many disabilities advocates, thinking VVPATs would be just like paper ballots, worried that voters would be required but unable to handle the paper themselves, so VVPATs became a security versus access issue for many.

Many disability rights advocates feared that counties would use DRE security issues to justify delaying making their polls and voting accessible. Attacking DREs for bad security was considered by some disabilities advocates as an attack on the access movement. (Actually, most of the concerns about DRE security problems come from computer scientists and transparent-voting advocates, not from foot-dragging counties.)

It is now clear that voter verification of the paper record is necessary to guarantee reliability and security. The only voting systems that permit truly accessible verification of the paper record are the ballot marking devices (BMDs, which are mechanical or computerized devices that help the voter mark votes on standard optical-scan paper ballots).

Hursti II, the Princeton University hack/virus demo, and other high-profile DRE security vulnerability revelations have forced many advocates for accessible voting to accept the need for security through paper ballots.

Like many others, most of us in the disability community trusted that "federal testing" would assure security and accessibility, but we eventually found that we'd been misled.

Many disability voting rights advocates now accept the notion that access and security are both important and not incompatible, and this is resulting in a slow but steady movement toward support of paper-ballot-based voting systems.

A Lack of Reliable Testing

Initially, with the passage of HAVA, many thought electronic voting systems would be great for reliability and accessibility.

Like many others, most of us in the disability community trusted that "federal testing" would assure security and accessibility, but we eventually found that we'd been misled. DREs did not turn out to be as secure, reliable or accessible as promised. And there turned out to be no actual "federal testing" by federal labs or "independent testing authorities" (ITAs). Instead, the "federal testing" was conducted by private labs that received payments from the voting machine vendors themselves, thereby creating an inherent conflict of interest.

Currently, there is no proper testing of the accessibility of voting machines, and there is no standard for comparison of results from accessibility, usability and accuracy testing.

Clearly, the ITA labs' testing of DREs and previous federal certification do not assure good disability accessibility compliance of a voting machine. . . .

I have had experience with the Sequoia Edge II DRE in five real-world elections in addition to testing most of the available voting systems at conferences, accessible voting equipment fairs and the NFB Baltimore accessible voting systems lab.

Note that the frequent mention of the Sequoia Edge II DRE voting system in this report is not meant to indicate that it is any better or worse than any other voting system. . . .

DREs Make Voting Difficult

March 2004 Election

In my first attempt to vote on a DRE in a real election, the poll workers were never able to get any of the machines at our polling place to boot with the audio assist feature working. After 45 minutes of struggling with the systems, the poll workers gave up and I had to have someone do my voting for me.

November 2004 Election

From the time I signed in and got my voter smart card, it took eight minutes to reboot the machine as an audio voting machine, 30 minutes to make my choices, 23 minutes to review and verify, and another four minutes to make a correction and record my vote. So in all, it took me about 65 minutes to mark and record my ballot. An added complication was that the ballot races on the Sequoia voting machine were not in the same order as those printed in the previously released public sample ballot.

November 2005 Election

The poll workers were unable to get the Sequoia machine booted up in the audio mode. After my wife borrowed the poll workers' operator's manual and figured out the correct audio boot process, she finally managed to get the machine properly rebooted and talking.

After 18 very frustrating minutes trying to get through the reboot process, it took about six minutes to fill out the eight choices on the very short ballot, seven minutes to review my vote, and another minute to record my ballot and finish. My total time working on the voting machine was 32 minutes.

Clearly, if I hadn't been very tenacious and taken my own computer expert along when I went to vote, I wouldn't have been able to vote privately.

June 2006 Election

For 12 minutes, the poll workers struggled repeatedly to program the voter ID card properly so it would cause my voting machine to talk. After they gave up, I was able to convince them that they were not encoding my voter ID card properly. Luckily, at the previous Voter Access Advisory Committee meeting, a member of the registrar of voters staff told me the trick to properly encoding the voter ID card for audio access mode.

After that, it took 31 minutes for me to navigate through the ballot-marking procedure. It then took eight more minutes for it to play out the ballot review. At this point, I decided that I needed to change one of my votes to a write-in, and that complicated and tedious procedure took another seven minutes.

By the time the Sequoia Edge II system printed the non-accessible paper trail and then spit out my voter ID card, I had spent a total of 59.5 minutes trying to vote privately.

November 2006 Election

This time the poll workers knew how to properly set up the audio mode, so it only took about eight minutes to switch the Sequoia to audio. This makes only two out of five times that our poll workers have been able to successfully set up the audio voting mode by themselves.

The audio vote casting took a total of one hour and 17 minutes at the machine, not counting the time waiting in line to get in.

DREs Are Too Complicated

Most of the voting-system manufacturers say they are working on making future improvements to the audio prompts and other capabilities of their DRE machines. This sounds good and should be encouraged. However, like the dual-switch input-control feature and other access options that have long been promised by several of these vendors, these features are still not available on most of our real voting systems in our real polling places today.

Clearly, most of these DREs were not designed correctly to be operated in the real world by normal poll workers and voters.

As my own experiences prove, it is certainly possible for some tenacious voters with disabilities to get through the voting process successfully on these voting systems. However, that experienced computer and access-technology users like myself have had such frustrating experiences trying to use the DRE voting systems clearly indicates that these systems have not been designed to provide appropriate access for the general population of voters with disabilities.

The problems that poll workers have had properly setting up the DRE voting systems for use by voters with disabilities show that the machines also are not designed properly for operation by the general population of poll workers. The problem is due to flaws in the human-factors design of the DREs and should not be blamed on either the poll workers' or the voters' lack of technical expertise or training. Clearly, most of these DREs were not designed correctly to be operated in the real world by normal poll workers and voters.

In general, the setup of these machines in audio access mode is still too complicated for the average poll worker, marking and reviewing the ballot is too complex and takes a very long time for the audio voter, the physical privacy shielding is much worse than it used to be with punch-card systems, and audio voters do not have any way of verifying the paper audit trail privately or otherwise.

DREs Are not Accessible

Most of the available DRE voting systems do not meet current HAVA and ADA [Americans with Disabilities Act] disability accommodation requirements and are far from being able to comply with the new Voluntary Voting System Guidelines. They are not accessible for significant numbers of individuals with disabilities for at least the following reasons:

1. The lack of a dual-switch input-control interface on systems such as Diebold AccuVote TSX and ES&S iVotronic. These systems are inaccessible to many voters with severe manual dexterity disabilities who are unable to use touch screens or tactile key inputs.

2. The inadequacy of most of the systems' audio access features for voters who are blind or have visual impairments, cognitive impairments, severe motor impairments or dyslexia. One of the results is that marking and reviewing the ballot takes an extremely long time for audio voters.

3. The lack of simultaneous and synchronized audio and visual outputs. These systems are inaccessible to many voters with visual impairments. For example, the failure of many of the DREs to accommodate elderly voters who have developed severe visual impairments with age but are unfamiliar with, and unable to cope with, audio-only access technology because they have had normal vision most of their lives.

4. The lack of voter-adjustable magnification, contrast and display color settings that can improve the readability of text on the video displays.

5. Confusing menu-selection systems that are difficult for people with cognitive disabilities to use effectively.

6. Almost all of the systems' blatant lack of adequate privacy curtains to prevent eavesdroppers from reading voters' selections on their visual displays. This violates, among other things, voters' constitutional rights to cast private and secret ballots.

7. The systems' lack of capability to allow voters with disabilities to select for themselves different access modes or features to provide accessibility without intervention from poll workers.

8. Lack of proper boosted audio output levels for voters with hearing impairments.

9. The inadequate tactile control keypads on most of the systems.

10. The requirement, on some electronic voting systems, of voters to manually handle paper ballots or voter ID cards, which may make it difficult or impossible for some voters with severe manual dexterity impairments to complete the voting process independently.

11. The verification of the VVPATs on the systems is inaccessible to many voters with visual or motor impairments and voters with special language needs so that these voters cannot personally verify the printout of VVPAT printers on the DRE systems.

In other words, a significant portion of citizens with disabilities or special language needs who attempt to cast their votes on these poorly designed voting machines will be unable to do so privately and independently.

11

Verified Paper Audit Trails Will Discriminate Against the Disabled

Christopher J. Dodd

Christopher J. Dodd is a U.S. senator from Connecticut. After the controversial 2000 presidential election, he authored the Help America Vote Act of 2002.

According to the Help America Vote Act (HAVA) of 2002, all Americans have the right to verify their votes before casting their ballots. Requiring that verification be done solely with paper, however, discriminates against people who cannot see or read and people who cannot handle paper because of physical limitations. Legislation requiring verified paper audit trails without requiring additional accommodations for the disabled to vote privately and independently would be in conflict with HAVA.

Mr. Chairman: I appreciate your calling this hearing today to allow the Committee to receive testimony about methods of providing for voter verification of ballots in federal elections. I also appreciate the opportunity this morning to listen to some very important witnesses and to colleagues who have introduced legislation on voter verification. The issue of voter verification has provoked some controversy across the country as to how you can verify your vote before it is cast.

I do not have any inherent objection at all to paper audits. My concern from the very outset in the drafting of election

Christopher J. Dodd, "Statement of Senator Christopher J. Dodd, United States House of Representatives, Committee on Rules and Administration, Hearing on Voter Verification in Federal Elections," rules.senate.gov, June 21, 2005.

reform legislation has been that there are millions of people in this country who are disabled—visually disabled, manually disabled, among other forms of disability. Some bills that are currently being considered exclude the ability of the disabled to vote privately and independently, at least it is perceived this way. For these millions of Americans who have never been able to vote privately and independently, for the first time under HAVA [Help America Vote Act], we guarantee that right. In the very first part of the bill, we guarantee that right.

HAVA Guarantees Voter Verification

We say in HAVA that every voter must have the right to verify their ballot before the ballot is cast, and I will read the specific line in a few minutes. But all the legislation or most of it that has been introduced excludes the ability of the disabled to have that same right. By insisting on paper, we are denying people who cannot read because they cannot see, or for reasons otherwise cannot manually operate the system a chance to verify what they have done. And I will just tell you here, I will vehemently oppose any legislation that excludes the ability of individuals with disabilities to have the right to do the same thing that those who can see and are manually dexterous have.

So to me, this need not be a battle. We made this a battle that need not exist, because I do not believe any of my colleagues—I do not want to believe—are going to endorse or support a piece of legislation that would disenfranchise disabled voters. After the Americans with Disabilities Act [law passed in 1990 prohibiting discrimination against individuals with physical or mental impairment], anyone who arrived in this building here this morning, took an elevator—unless you walked up the stairs—to get to the third floor, and you could not see and you pushed a button, you would know that there is braille on that elevator. We require it under the law.

There are curb cutouts that make it possible for people who cannot walk to get on the sidewalk. Do you think we are going to pass legislation to allow people to vote and not give them the opportunity to do so privately and independently? It is not going to happen, in my view. So my concern is whether or not we are going to make it possible. With all the talk about paper, I am fine; but the problem is that I want to also guarantee that those Americans who cannot see and cannot operate those machines are going to have the same opportunity to verify their ballots.

If you use paper to verify your votes, then you must also guarantee that the disabled will have the opportunity to verify their votes.

As the Senate author of the Help America Vote Act, my position in support of voter verified ballots has been indisputable from the time I introduced comprehensive election reform legislation in 2001. . . . After conference with the House, that bill became the Help America Vote Act of 2002, or HAVA, as we call it.

This legislation that I authored required, for the first time in our nation's history, that all voting systems used in federal elections meet certain requirements. The very first requirement of my bill, S.565, was, and I will quote it here:

> The voting system shall permit the voter to verify the votes selected by the voter on a ballot before the ballot is cast and tabulated, and shall provide the voter with the opportunity to correct any error before the ballot is cast and tabulated.

And that requirement is now the law of the land. As enacted in HAVA, the states must comply with that requirement by January 1 of [2006].

So I will take a backseat to absolutely no one when it comes to support of voter verified ballots.

Moreover, HAVA requires that every voting system that is used in a federal election produce a permanent paper record with a manual audit capacity for that system. That is the law.

But what HAVA did not require was a one-size-fits all solution as to how voter verification of the ballot was reduced to a permanent paper record. Quite frankly, that is a technology issue that Congress, in my view, is ill-equipped to decide. . . .

So I take great offense at any suggestion that I oppose either a voter verified ballot or a paper record of such ballot. But let me make clear my position: I not only disdain, but categorically reject, any voting system, including one that requires a voter verified paper audit trail, that is not fully accessible to the disabled as required by federal law under HAVA.

We have come too far in this country to disregard the needs of millions of our fellow citizens.

Voting Must Be Accessible to All

This need not be a choice of paper over the disabled. The disabled community does not object to the use of paper to verify a voter's decision. They insist, however, and I will insist, that if you use paper to verify your votes, then you must also guarantee that the disabled will have the opportunity to verify their votes. For the blind, this means an audio system; for the manually disabled, an accommodation must be made. The Americans with Disabilities Act certainly requires nothing less. As I mentioned a few moments ago, we have accommodated the disabled, who are 20 percent of the population of this country.

It is not just a tiny percentage of the population. Twenty percent of our fellow citizens are disabled and require accommodation in this process. As I mentioned earlier, today we require that a simple thing like an elevator be accessible. The idea that the most fundamental right that we have in this country, the right to vote and to choose our representatives, would not be as accessible as a curb or an elevator ought to offend every single one of us.

The idea that we are going to have a paper audit trail or a paper verification system and disregard 20 percent of our fellow citizens ought to offend every citizen of this country, and it certainly does this one. And so, I will insist that as we go forward here, any effort to make this a one size fits all solution that discriminates against people who are disabled, I will vehemently, vehemently oppose, and I hope others would join me in that effort.

My position is clear, consistent and unambiguous: I support voter verification, including voter verified audit trails, so long as all aspects of the voting system, including the permanent audit record, are accessible to voters with disabilities and language minorities. The ATM machine is cited all the time. You can go to an ATM machine, and you get an audio system that will tell you what transaction you have just engaged in, as well as having a paper trail, if you will.

But I will continue to oppose reducing individual voter verification to an inaccessible paper-only method as the solution. We have come too far in this country to disregard the needs of millions of our fellow citizens. They should be able to cast a vote private and independently. . . .

I am not opposed to states requiring a voter verified audit trail—the provision I authored in HAVA already requires that states establish a permanent paper record with audit capacity for election systems.

But I am opposed to federally mandating that states implement voter verification by means of a paper record *only*. Regrettably, that is what the legislation proposed last year required, and that is what some legislation reintroduced this Congress requires. Such a requirement would discriminate against the disabled and those who are language minorities and the illiterate.

Technology has not yet produced a paper record that is fully accessible to everyone, and as long as I am a member of this body, I will oppose any attempt to reduce voter verification to a piece of paper that is inaccessible to the disability community. . . .

Technology may eventually provide us an answer. I believe it will. But today, voter verification must include alternatives to paper and systems that do not require the disabled to seek assistance in either the casting or verification of their ballot. States that require otherwise risk being in violation of federal law.

The provisions of HAVA are very clear on this point. Section 301 of HAVA requires that the voting system be accessible for individuals with disabilities, including nonvisual access for the blind and visually impaired, in a manner that provides the same opportunity for access and participation as other voters—and here I quote: "Including privacy and independence."

What that means is that any state that chooses to add a voter verified audit trail as part of their voting system must make that audit trail accessible to the disabled in an manner that allows the disabled to verify their choices in an independent and private manner.

The blind cannot verify their choices by means of a piece of paper alone in a manner that is either independent or private. Nor can an individual who has a mobility disability, such as hand limitations, verify a piece of paper alone, if that individual is required to pick up and handle the paper.

Alternatives to Paper Verification

Consequently, a state that chooses to require a voter verified paper audit trail must also provide a means for the disabled to privately and independently access and verify that paper.

For the blind and visually impaired, that may mean adding an audio or non-visual system that can "read" the paper audit trail back to the voter. In the case of an individual who has hand limitations, the system would have to provide a means of accessing the paper audit trail without having to actually pick up the paper or manipulate it.

Technology affords us the opportunity to make voting accessible to all persons with disabilities, and HAVA establishes the civil right of all disabled individuals to cast a ballot in a private and independent manner.

Congress has appropriated $3 billion to date to assist the states in implementing disabled accessible systems. The states simply have no excuse for purchasing voting systems that are not accessible to the disabled.

The language of HAVA is clear: states may choose whatever voting system they please to comply with the law. But, what is equally clear is that whatever system a state chooses to implement, *all* components of that voting system, including any audit trail information, under section 301 (b) of the law, must meet the requirements of HAVA, specifically, the disabled and language minority accessibility requirements. . . .

I would just mention in closing, when I raised and discussed this issue over the last year or so with people who have talked on this subject, on several occasions I have heard people say—you know, it is just tough, maybe the disabled are just going to have to be inconvenienced a bit. I am using the words, quoting by the way, "inconvenienced a little bit." Anyone who has had any contact with people knows what it means to be inconvenienced if you are disabled.

We have fought very hard to pass a very good bill, a bipartisan bill, a strong bill. For the very first time in our 218 year history, the federal government has gotten involved in the conduct of federal elections, other than the Voting Rights Act back in 1964 which said what could not be done with poll taxes and literacy tests. With HAVA, we said what you must do as well, and that is to make elections fair and equal and accessible and set up better systems as a result of the debacle we saw in 2000 and to some degree in 2004. It is not a perfect piece of legislation, but it is the [basis for] the federal government being involved in federal elections. We have a lot more to do to get this right, but I hope we can resolve this matter between paper and the disabled community and not end up having a battle in this country that need not be waged.

12

Electronic Voting Should Be Continued

Ernie Tedeschi

Ernie Tedeschi is a graduate student in the master's of public policy program at the Goldman School of Public Policy at the University of California, Berkeley. He is a frequent contributor to the journal PolicyMatters. *He is interested in urban policy, social equity, and military issues.*

Electric voting machines known as direct-recording electronic voting systems (DREs) are not only fast, they also offer the best system for registering voter preference. Although DREs have some drawbacks such as size, expense, and security, American technology is capable of fixing these issues. The machines should continue to be used because of their increased accuracy in reporting election results.

L ike a barbarian horde gathered at the city gates, journalists around the world were ready to pounce at the opportunity to blame electronic voting machines—used in 38% of American jurisdictions on Election Day—for irregularities in the midterm elections [November 2006]. In the week before Election Day, the *Pittsburgh Post-Gazette* editorialized about the "Fear of Vote Fraud" while *The New York Times* ran an article titled "In the Land of 'Every Vote Counts,' Uncertainty on Whether It's Counted Correctly." Even the international press couldn't resist: the British *Observer* proclaimed "Just Hack Your Way to Victory, Mr. President," while the *Irish Times*

Ernie Tedeschi, "In Defense of Electronic Voting Machines," *PolicyMatters*, vol. 4, autumn 2006, pp. 40–42. Reproduced by permission.

went with a more measured "E-vote of Confidence No Shoo-in." American democracy itself seemed on the brink of collapse.

The result must have sorely disappointed the doomsayers. Besides the smattering of alleged tally irregularities in a few districts with razor-thin races, the electronic voting machine Class of 2006 has yet to face the same firestorm of criticisms, both valid and frankly paranoid, that stemmed from the 2004 Presidential election. Cleveland's *Plain Dealer* summarized Tuesday's test of electronic voting machines thusly: "Still imperfect, but much better." The *Washington Post* agreed, saying "[t]he system worked." The republic, it seems, may endure another two years after all.

The failure of an electoral apocalypse should be little comfort to Americans, however. Electronic voting machines have not redeemed themselves quite yet. Beneath the conspiracy theories posted daily in the blogosphere lay legitimate flaws in both the hardware and software of these systems that have yet to be addressed. Now is not the time to be complacent. Rather, as I imagine the Republican Party is doing with its own organization right this minute, we need to revisit the core principles of electronic voting, remind ourselves of its lofty promises, and review where the machines went critically wrong. In short, we should become born-again electronic voters.

Electronic Voting Machines Are Worth It

With the national dialogue consumed by serious allegations against electronic voting machines, a quick reevaluation of why, exactly, state officials thought these machines were such a good idea in the first place is in order.

First, a bit of context. When we refer to "electronic voting machines," what we usually mean are direct-recording electronic (DRE) voting systems, those touch-screen units you've likely seen on the news or on the Internet. The optical scan ballots we use here in Alameda County, California, as well as the old punch-card ballots, are also counted by computer. But, because the inputs are paper ballots, election experts classify them in a different category from DRE machines, which store voter selections electronically.

Therein lies the first major advantage of DRE systems over optical scan ballots: speed and accuracy in the end-count. When each precinct delivers its DRE election data to county offices at the end of the day, the tally is nearly instantaneous and a 100% accurate reflection of what the precinct officer delivered. Admittedly, however, machines that cost between $3,000 and $4,000 per unit, as the flagship DRE systems do right now, ought to deliver more substantive advantages than speed and a marginal increase in end-count accuracy.

As it turns out, DRE systems offer the best hope to date of addressing a fundamental problem endemic to democracy since the invention of the secret ballot. The flaw is called "residual voting," and refers to those cases when human error prevents a ballot from accurately reflecting the voter's true electoral preferences. The reason we ought to be concerned about residual voting is that, often times, the limitations of the ballot medium (paper) or indeed the very ballot design itself (think of the "butterfly" ballots in the 2000 election) can encourage these errors.

The Problem of Overvoting and Undervoting

The two most problematic varieties of residual voting are over- and under-voting. Over-voting occurs when a person marks off more candidates than she is supposed to, such as voting for two presidential candidates. Under-voting is a bit harder to measure: it happens when a voter misses a race on the ballot for which she otherwise has a preference and doesn't mark a vote. In a country so closely divided, where many elections deliver a margin of victory less than the margin of error, lost residual votes are far from insignificant. MIT political scientist Charles Stewart estimates the nationwide rate of under-voting at 1.9% in the 2000 election, or about 2.3 million votes.

A DRE America would effectively enfranchise 250,000–800,000 more people.

DRE systems address over-voting in the most straightforward way possible: the software simply won't allow you to vote for more than the allowed number of choices. The DRE prescription for under-voting is, like the problem itself, less concrete but, short a psychic in every polling place, it's the best solution to date. Since most DRE machines go one-by-one through each race on the ballot and require voters to actively choose to move on to the next race, we can be confident that a voter who submits a ballot has reviewed all the races and issues. Our confidence can only be strengthened by those DRE machines with voter-verified paper receipts, offering another opportunity for ballot review.

The benefit of DREs, then, is manifest: Stewart found that after applying statistical controls, jurisdictions that adopted DRE voting systems after 2000 saw a 33–100% greater decline in residual voting rates than those that either adopted optical scan systems or didn't change systems at all.

That deserves emphasis: DRE voting machines are *more* accurate at registering voter preferences than optical scan systems. If you scaled Stewart's findings nationwide, a DRE America would effectively enfranchise 250,000–800,000 more people. That potential alone makes electronic voting machines worth consideration.

The Help America Vote Act and DREs

It's unfortunate that with so much that DRE systems could make better about American elections, voting machine firms found ways of making them worse. For this, the state and federal governments deserve some blame. The Help America Vote Act (HAVA), passed by Congress in 2002, allocated $650 million to local jurisdictions to replace antiquated voting equipment in the wake of the 2000 election. States passed their own spending bills to augment federal generosity; Californians, for example, approved in Proposition 41 a $200 million bond the same year that HAVA was enacted. Since these funds were available on a first-come, first-served basis, counties had an incentive to upgrade their voting systems as quickly as possible.

The problem was that America's voting machine firms weren't ready. Now-notorious Diebold had developed ATM-like technology for Brazilian elections that performed brilliantly. However, these machines were ill-equipped to handle the needs of U.S. jurisdictions, where ballot regulations differed from state to state and the ballot measures themselves came in almost every imaginable variety. Anticipating the government largesse of HAVA, Diebold bought Global Electronic Systems of McKinney, Texas—and with it their AccuVote TS model—for $30 million in June 2001. Unfortunately, the AccuVote TS was, like almost all electronic voting machines at the time, essentially a first-generation system. It was a small Texas company's first crack at the burgeoning electronic voting market and exemplified the problems common to almost all the DRE systems available then and, unbelievably, still today.

First, DREs tend to be both heavy and bulky. The AccuVote TSx, Diebold's latest incarnation of the line, weighs in at 26 lbs. Sequoia's AVC Edge is an even more unmanageable 40 lbs. Even Election System & Software's iVotronic, the industry's lightest machine at 15 lbs, is almost three times as heavy as the average laptop computer. Given the computer industry's amazing success in cramming more computing power into progressively smaller packages, the sheer mass of these systems is unforgivable. Weighty computers are not only harder to set up, especially for elderly poll workers, but they prove less accessible for disabled voters who need ballots brought to their cars.

Second, DRE machines are expensive, and this leads to polling congestion. Most of the long lines in DRE precincts are not due to computer malfunctions; they're due to the fact that, at $4,000 a unit, most jurisdictions can't afford to set up the same number of DRE polling stations as they did punch-card polling stations in years past. When Santa Clara County in California bought 5,000 Sequoia AVC Edges in 2003, they effectively reduced the number of polling stations per precinct by almost half.

It would be a tragedy for our democracy if America let the perfect be the enemy of the good and wrote off electronic voting machines entirely.

Thirdly, and most importantly, there's the issue of security. To their credit, all three of the nation's biggest voting machine firms now offer voter-verified paper trails as a peripheral to their flagship systems, and this move has addressed some of the integrity concerns raised by computer scientists over the years. There is still, however, insufficient oversight given to each machine's source code. Most firms hold their systems' machine and source codes in escrow, which is in practice little different from keeping them secret. The drawback to this approach is a lack of transparency, which not only depresses voter confidence in the integrity of their vote, but also lowers the likelihood that malicious code written by someone within the firm will be detected.

Problems Can Be Fixed

In the end, though, we can address each and every one of these problems. An industry on the verge of selling ultramobile PCs weighing less than 2 lbs. each and priced under $1,500 is certainly capable of developing secure voting solutions both portable and affordable to local jurisdictions. However, because jurisdictions that purchase these machines presumably will only do so only once every 15 years or more, we cannot rely on steady and consistent consumption to eventually yield reliable voting machines. We instead need to provide incentives to mobilize America's wealth of computer talent. A large monetary prize awarded to the firm or individual who designs a voting machine that is at once lightweight, inexpensive, and secure, would be an appropriate entrepreneurial solution.

The problems with DRE machines certainly deserve prompt action. But it's a bit ironic that the most frequent charge against them is their openness to manipulation when, in an era of gerrymandering, push-polls, and deceptive campaign advertising, DRE systems are one of the few political innovations in recent years that aim to increase the accuracy with which we record voter preferences. It would be a tragedy for our democracy if America let the perfect be the enemy of the good and wrote off electronic voting machines entirely.

Organizations to Contact

The editors have compiled the following list of organizations concerned with the issues debated in this book. The descriptions are derived from materials provided by the organizations. All have publications or information available for interested readers. The list was compiled on the date of publication of the present volume; the information provided here may change. Be aware that many organizations take several weeks or longer to respond to inquiries, so allow as much time as possible.

American Association of People with Disabilities (AAPD)
1629 K Street NW, Suite 503, Washington, DC   20006
(800) 840-8844
Web site: www.aapd-dc.org

The AAPD strives to provide economic and political equity for all people with disabilities. Through its Disability Vote Project, the AAPD works to make sure that all disabled voters are able to fully access polling places and voting equipment. AAPD is in favor of electronic voting. Its Web site provides news, personal stories, and updates on the status of voting for the disabled.

The Association for Computing Machinery (ACM)
2 Penn Plaza, Suite 701, New York, NY   10121-0701
(800) 342-6626 • fax: (212) 869-0481
e-mail: USACM_DC@acm.org
Web site: www.acm.org

The ACM is an international scientific and educational organization dedicated to advancing the arts, sciences, and applications of information technology. The ACM provides useful resources regarding the technological issues of electronic voting. Its Web site contains hundreds of full text articles and comments concerning the actual voting machinery.

Black Box Voting (BBV)
330 SW forty-third Street, Suite K   PMB 547
(206) 335-7747
e-mail: crew@blackboxvoting.org
Web site: www.blackboxvoting.org

BBV is a nonpartisan, nonprofit organization. Founded by journalist and consumer advocate Bev Harris, Black Box Voting calls itself "America's Elections Watchdog Group." The organization is opposed to electronic voting on the grounds that electronic voting is neither transparent nor secure. Publications available through its Web site include the twenty-module *Citizen's Tool Kit* and the complete text of Bev Harris's book, *Black Box Voting: Ballot Tampering in the 21st Century*.

The California Voter Foundation (CVF)
2612 J Street, Suite 8, Sacramento, CA   95816
(916) 441-2494
Web site: www.calvoter.org

The CVF is a nonprofit, nonpartisan organization promoting and applying the responsible use of technology to improve the democratic process. It is concerned with the places where democracy and technology intersect, such as in electronic voting. Its Web site offers publications on campaign disclosures, voter engagement, voter privacy, and voting technology.

Common Cause
1133 Nineteenth Street, NW Ninth Floor
Washington, DC   20036
(202) 833-1200
Web site: www.commoncause.org

Common Cause is an advocacy organization whose stated purpose is to serve as a vehicle for citizens to make their voices heard in the political process and to hold their elected leaders accountable to the public interest. Common Cause is currently working on several issues: increasing diversity within the media, advancing campaign reform, ensuring openness and accountability in government, increasing participation in the political process, removing barriers to voting, and ensuring that voting systems are accurate and accessible. Common Cause's Web site provides numerous articles on electronic voting and a comprehensive FAQ list on the subject. In addition, the Web site offers a blog that includes comments on legal challenges to e-voting.

The Election Center:
The National Association of Election Officials
12543 Westella, Suite 100, Houston, TX   77077
(281) 293-0101 • fax (281) 293-0453
e-mail: services@electioncenter.org
Web site: www.electioncenter.org

The Election Center is a nonprofit organization whose members are nearly all governmental employees whose duties include voter registration and elections administration. It offers training, education, and resources for its members on technology and legislation. Publications include task force reports as well as op-ed articles and governmental testimony on voting issues.

The Electronic Frontier Foundation (EFF)
454 Shotwell Street, San Francisco, CA   94110-1914
(454) 436-9333 • fax: (415) 436-9993
e-mail: information@eff.org
Web site: www.eff.org

The EFF is a nonprofit organization whose stated purpose is to defend freedom in the digital world. Largely through court cases, the EFF defends free speech, privacy, and consumers' rights. In addition, the EFF maintains an advocacy action center comprised of like-minded citizens working to educate the public and lawmakers. One of main topics concerning the EFF currently is e-voting. Its Web site maintains a full listing of court cases involving their advocacy as well as news items and press releases.

FairVote

6930 Carroll Avenue, Suite 610, Takoma Park, MD   20912
(301) 270-4616 • fax: (301) 270-4133
Web site: www.fairvote.org

FairVote, formerly known as the Center for Voting and Democracy, is an advocacy group whose goals include achieving the following election reforms: a constitutionally protected right to vote, direct election of the president, instant runoff voting for executive elections, and proportional voting for legislative elections. FairVote publishes research reports, policy perspectives, and democracy innovations; these are available on its Web site and in hard copy from the Web site bookstore.

Federal Election Commission (FEC)

999 E Street, NW, Washington, DC   20463
(800) 424-9530
Web site: www.fec.gov

The FEC was created in 1975 to administer and enforce the Federal Election Campaign Act. The commission is bipartisan and is comprised of six members, appointed by the president of the United States. It is an independent regulatory agency charged with overseeing the funding of presidential elections as well as enforcing the provisions of the law concerning contributions to candidates. The FEC maintains its twenty-year and thirty-year reports as well as summaries of meetings on its Web site.

League of Women Voters (LWV)

1730 M Street NW, Suite 1000, Washington, DC   20036-4508
(202) 429-1965 • fax: (202) 429-0854
Web site: www.lwv.org

The LWV is a nonpartisan, political organization whose mission is to encourage informed and active participation in government, to work to increase understanding of major public policy issues, and to influence public policy through education and advocacy. In recent years, the league has internally debated the role of verified paper audit trails. Its Web site is searchable and hosts many excellent articles on electronic voting and on voting in general.

National Committee for Voting Integrity (NCVI)
1718 Connecticut Ave, NW, Suite 200
Washington, DC   20009
(202) 483-1140, ext. 111 • fax: (202) 483-1248
Web site: www.votingintegrity.org

The NCVI is a project of the Electronic Privacy Information Center. The NCVI brings together experts on voting issues from across the United States to promote discussion among computer scientists, election administrators, voting rights advocates, policy makers, the media, and the public on methods to ensure fair, reliable, secure, accurate, accountable, and auditable public elections. Its Web site offers information on each type of voting technology, on laws affecting voting, on voting rights, and on voting security issues.

Open Voting Consortium (OVC)
9560 Windrose Lane, Granite Bay, CA   95746
(916) 772-5360
e-mail: alan@openvoting.org
Web site: www.openvotingconsortium.org

The OVC is a nonprofit organization comprised of computer science professionals who are devoted to developing electronic voting technology that will provide safe, accountable, and verifiable election results. It lobbies for legislation in support of open source software voting systems and holds public education and media events to speak on these issues. Its Web site provides a FAQ list on open voting systems as well as a collection of news articles concerning electronic voting.

The Pacific Research Institute (PRI)
755 Sansome Street, Suite 450, San Francisco, CA   94111
(415) 989-0833 • fax: (415) 989-2411
e-mail: info@pacificresearch.org

Web site: www.pacificresearch.org

The PRI is a conservative think tank dedicated to free-market policy. PRI publishes books and papers in public policy areas such as education, environment, health care, and technology. The PRI technology researchers have addressed electronic voting and released a comprehensive study defending electronic voting, available on the Web site. In addition, the fully searchable Web site has full-text articles from a variety of sources concerning electronic voting.

The United States Election Assistance Commission (EAC)
1225 New York Avenue NW, Suite 1100
Washington, DC   20005
(866) 747-1471 • fax: (202) 566-3127
e-mail: HAVAinfo@eac.gov
Web site: www.eac.gov

The EAC was established by the Help America Vote Act of 2002. The job of the EAC is to serve as a national clearinghouse and information resource and to review administrative procedures of federal elections. The EAC has been the agency largely responsible for the oversight of electronic voting. On its Web site, the EAC maintains a long list of publications, a FAQ list, a database of news and communications, and a list of election resources.

Verified Voting Foundation
1550 Bryant Street, Suite 855, San Francisco, CA   94103
(415) 487-2255 • fax (940) 403-2255
Web site: www.verifiedvotingfoundation.org

Verified Voting Foundation is an organization whose stated mission is to educate the public about electronic voting. Founded by Stanford University computer science professor David Dill, the organization advocates for required voter-verified paper ballots on electronic voting machines. Its Web site provides full-text, up-to-date news articles and summaries of legislation, policy, and litigation regarding electronic voting.

VotersUnite.Org
3417 NW Donida Drive, Bremerton, WA   98312
e-mail: vucontact@votersunite.org
Web site: www.votersunite.org

VotersUnite.Org is a nonpartisan, national grass-roots advocacy organization whose members believe that electronic voting cannot provide fair and accurate elections. It collects, publishes, and distributes incidents reported by poll workers, voters, and media concerning problems with electronic voting. It offers two free downloadable booklets on its Web site, *E-Voting Failures in the 2006 Mid-Term Elections: A Sampling of Problems Across the Nation*, and *Myth Breakers: Facts about Electronic Elections*, second edition.

Bibliography

Books

Alan Abramowitz	*Voice of the People: Elections and Voting in the United States.* New York: McGraw-Hill, 2004.
Mark A. Abramson and Therese L. Morin	*E-government 2003.* Lanham, MD: Rowman & Littlefield, 2003.
R. Michael Alvarez and Thad E. Hall	*Point, Click and Vote: The Future of Internet Voting.* Washington, DC: Brookings, 2004.
David Card and Enrico Moretti	*Does Voting Technology Affect Election Outcomes? Touch-Screen Voting and the 2004 Presidential Election.* Cambridge, MA: National Bureau of Economic Research, 2005.
Richard F. Celeste and Dick Thornburgh	*Asking the Right Questions about Electronic Voting.* Washington, DC: National Academies, 2006.
Kevin J. Coleman, and Richard M. Nunno	*Internet Voting: Issues and Legislation.* Washington, DC: Congressional Research Service, Library of Congress, 2002.
Abbe Waldman DeLozier and Vickie Karp	*Hacked! High Tech Election Theft in America: 11 Experts Expose the Truth.* Austin, TX: Truth Enterprises, 2006.

Eric A. Fischer   *Election Reform and Electronic Voting systems (DREs): Analysis of Security Issues.* Washington, DC: Congressional Research Service, Library of Congress; Penny Hill, 2003.

Steven F. Freeman   *Was the 2004 Presidential Election Stolen? Exit Polls, Election Fraud, and the Official Count.* New York: Seven Stories, 2006.

Donald Green   *Get Out the Vote!: How To Increase Voter Turnout.* Washington, DC: Brookings, 2004.

Dimitris Gritzalis, ed.   *Secure Electronic Voting (Advances in Information Security).* New York: Springer, 2003.

Andrew Gumbel   *Steal This Vote: Dirty Elections and the Rotten History of Democracy in America.* New York: Nation Books, 2005.

Bev Harris   *Black Box Voting: Ballot Tampering in the 21st Century.* Renton, WA: Talion, 2004.

Paul S. Herrnson, Richard G. Niemi, and Michael J. Hanmer   *Voting Technology: The Not-So-Simple Act of Casting a Ballot.* Washington, DC: Brookings, 2007.

Norbert Kersting and Harald Baldersheim   *Electronic Voting and Democracy: A Comparative Analysis.* New York: Palgrave Macmillan, 2004.

Paul McCaffrey, ed.   *U.S. Election System.* New York: H.W. Wilson, 2004.

Geralyn Miller   *Changing the Way America Votes: Election Reform, Incrementalism, and Cutting Deals.* Lewiston, NY: Edwin Mellen, 2004.

Aviel D. Rubin   *Brave New Ballot: The Battle to Safeguard Democracy in the Age of Electronic Voting.* New York: Morgan Road Books, 2006.

Roy G. Saltman   *The History and Politics of Voting Technology: In Quest of Integrity and Public Confidence.* New York: Palgrave Macmillan, 2006.

Tova Wang   *Understanding the Debate over Electronic Voting Machine.* New York: Century Foundation, 2004.

Periodicals

Cameron W. Barr   "Security of Electronic Voting Is Condemned; Paper Systems Should Be Included, Agency Says," *Washington Post*, December 1, 2006.

David Batstone   "The Machine Ate My Vote: E-Voting May Make Us Nostalgic for Hanging Chads," *Soujourners*, September 1, 2004.

Silla Brush   "Election Corrections," *U.S. New & World Report*, July 17, 2006.

Business Wire   "The Legal Center Announces Greater Accessibility for Voters with Disabilities on Nov. 7," October 26, 2004.

Massimo Calabresi — "The Wizard of Odd: Electronic Voting Machines and the Blogger Brett Kimberline," *Time*, January 15, 2007.

Adam Cohen — "The Good News (Really) about Voting Machines," *New York Times*, January 10, 2007.

Adam Cohen — "What's Wrong with My Voting Machine," *New York Times*, December 4, 2006.

Catherine Dolinski — "Gambling on Votes? Experts Say You Do," *Tampa Tribune*, December 15, 2006.

Adam Friedman — "The Internet's Potential to Affect Social Studies and Democracy," *International Journal of Social Education*, Spring–Summer 2006.

Barney Gimbel — "Rage against the Machine," *Fortune*, November 13, 2006.

Thomas C. Greene — "E-Voting Security: Getting It Right," *Register*, July 8, 2004.

Kurt Hyde — "Saving Our Elections: America's Once Proud and Trustworthy Elections Are Being Undermined, but Concerned Citizens Can Take Steps to Restore the Integrity of Our Electoral Process," *New American*, October 30, 2006.

Anna Kaplan — "Follow the Nonexistent Paper Trail," *Humanist*, January–February 2005.

Phil Keisling   "Internet Voting? A Technology Too Far," *American Prospect*, May 2006.

Steven Levy   "Will Your Vote Count in 2006?" *Newsweek*, May 29, 2006.

Sarah F. Liebschutz and Daniel J. Palazzolo   "HAVA and the States," *Publius*, Fall 2005.

Mark Crispin Miller   "None Dare Call It Stolen," *Harpers*, August 2005.

Michael Niman   "A Brave New World of Voting," *Humanist*, January–February 2004.

Wayne M. O'Leary   "It's Time to Pull the Plug on High-Tech Voting Systems," *Portland Press Herald/Maine Sunday Telegram*, February 11, 2007.

Ben Rothke   "Like Elections, E-Voting Must Be Open," *Computerworld*, January 8, 2007.

Tim Storey   "Helping America Vote: After More than 200 Years of Voting, the United States Is about to Make a Massive Investment in the Neglected Elections Infrastructure," *State Legislatures*, April 1, 2003.

Daniel P. Tokaji   "The Paperless Chase: Electronic Voting and Democratic Values," *Fordham Law Review*, March 2005.

George F. Will   "Who Needs to 'Help' America Vote?" *Washington Post*, October 29, 2006.

Elizabeth M. Yang and Kristi Gaines — "Voting Technology and the Law: From Chads to Fads and Somewhere in Between," *Social Education*, October 1, 2004.

Jeanne Zaino — "A New Era in Voting Technology: The Changing Landscape of Election Disputes," *Dispute Resolution Journal*, August–October 2004.

Internet Sources

Debra D'Agostino — "E-Voting: Will Your Vote Count?" *CIO Insight*, August 11, 2006. www.cioinsight.com.

Marc Fisher — "If Paper Ballots Restore Trust in Elections, Let's Switch," *Washington Post*, September 21, 2006. www.washingtonpost.com.

Farhad Manjoo — "Hacking Democracy," *Salon.com*, February 20, 2003. http://dir.salon.com.

Avi Rubin — "Low Tech Is the Answer," *Business Week Online*, October 30, 2006. www.businessweek.com.

Ellen Theisen — "Myth Breakers: Facts about Electronic Elections," *VotersUnite.Org*, 2006. www.VotersUnite.Org.

Kim Zetter — "How E-Voting Threatens Democracy," *Wired News*, March 29, 2004. www.wired.com.

Index